Pantry Raid

out of the cupboard cooking

foreword by Elizabeth Baird

Dana McCauley

whitecap

To Martin and Oliver, my ever-willing guinea pigs,
comic advisers and candid (but usually kind) critics.

Whitecap Books
Vancouver/Toronto

Edited by Alison Maclean
Proofread by Lesley Cameron
Cover and interior design by Maxine Lea
Cover photographs by Christopher Freeland
Interior illustrations by Joanna Mitchell

Food Photographs by
Christopher Freeland: Sushi Stack Canapés, Asian Glazed Pork Rolls, Beautiful Beet Borscht,
Green Goddess Dressing and Dip, Fall Greens with Roasted Tomatoes, Cheese and Cracker Chicken,
Lime-Glazed Scallops on Creamy Wasabi Fettucine, Twenty-Minute Linguine with Clam Sauce,
Maple-Glazed Carrots, Tuscan Green Bean Salad
Michael Kohn: Grilled Shrimp Cocktail
Michael Visser: Vineyard Chicken Salad, Caesar Salad Sandwich
Douglas Bradshaw: Luau Rice
Rob Fiocca: Cheesy Polenta Surprise
Robert Wiginton: Citrus Compote

Printed and bound in Canada

National Library of Canada Cataloguing in Publication Data

McCauley, Dana.
Pantry raid

Includes index.
ISBN 1-55285-333-0

1. Quick and easy cookery. I. Title.
TX833.5.M32 2002   641.5'55   C2002-910017-8

The publisher acknowledges the support of the Canada Council for the Arts and the Cultural Services
Branch of the Government of British Columbia for our publishing program. We acknowledge the financial
support of the Government of Canada through the Book Publishing Industry Development Program for
our publishing activities.

Contents

Acknowledgements

Pantry Raid, like most cookbooks, I suspect, has been an adventure to create. During the process the title of this book has changed at least three times and the recipes have been shuffled into different chapter categories as the book evolved and assumed shape. Needless to say, there have been good days and there have been bad days.

Throughout this progression I have received tremendous support from a number of people, including Alison Maclean who edited the book with an astonishingly keen eye and offered her well-considered insights just when they were needed the most. Whitecap's director of publishing Robert McCullough's support of this project has been most remarkable since he chose twice to include this book in Whitecap's line-up. (What can I say? I have a fickle streak.) Robert, I owe you a double helping of thanks!

Others who shared their opinions and wisdom as I wrote *Pantry Raid* include my husband and fellow chef Martin Kouprie, my food friend and colleague Adrian Doran, and photographer Chris Freeland who was instrumental in making this book easy on the eyes.

Appreciation also goes out to cookbook expert Alison Fryer who reviewed my original proposal and offered informed suggestions, and to Monda Rosenberg who commiserated with me when I needed it most. I also owe Elizabeth Baird a lifetime supply of jellied salads for the outstanding introduction she wrote to this book.

In the test kitchen, *Pantry Raid* profited from the culinary know-how of a trio of trusted and patient recipe testers, Tracey Syvret, Amy Snider and Kate Millman. Kathleen Harrison, Nadia Di Egidio and Dawn Bone tied on aprons to help with testing, too.

Likewise, valued tasters the Flynns, the Pacinis, Angie and Alexandra McNeill, Jeanne McCauley (and her bridge pals!) as well as the staff and students of Children's Académie Nursery School offered feedback and practical insights about many of the recipes in this book. Thanks to all of you for returning the dishes clean!

My thanks also to Dianne Rinehart, editor of *Homemaker's Magazine*, and to Margaret Hudson, director of sales and marketing for Burnbrae Farms Ltd. These ladies inspired me to create some of the recipes included in this book for projects I worked on with them.

Finally, a grateful nod is owed to Laurie McPhail, a friend of a friend who offered the name for this book. Although Laurie's wit wasn't instantly embraced by everyone, *Pantry Raid* seemed perfect to me the minute I heard it.

— Dana McCauley
   January 2002

Foreword

A few years back when Dana McCauley was a chef in the *Canadian Living* Test Kitchen, and mastering the art of recipe writing, she joked that perhaps we might just get away with saying "Cook until done," trusting that the person holding the whisk would recognize "doneness" when it appeared.

And how exactly could that cook, recipe in hand and in the midst of making a beurre blanc, tell when it was done? Dana figured out the wording, of course, and over the last seven years has just got better and better at telling people not only how to tell when "it's done," but also all the prepping and cooking steps that lead up to the magic moment when she has you, the reader/cook, ready to swirl the sauce out of the pan and over the perfectly cooked salmon. That is, with just a hint of coral color inside. Applause, please, from those assembled around the table!

Dana takes the cook one step further in *Pantry Raid*, a collection of more than 200 everyday and entertaining recipes remarkable in their contemporary flair and restaurant chef pizzazz but with the solid underpinnings of home cook make-ability. She confidently leads right into the heart of cooking—planning what to stock in the pantry so the foundation is laid for fuss-free cooking. None of that frazzled end-of-day, end-of-wits torture that leads people like zombies to the prepared food counter at the supermarket or, heaven forbid, dialing for take-out. A well- stocked pantry turns into a friend whose support is essential in turning out delicious meals for weeknight and weekend.

She guides the reader as a friend, using one of the clearest and easiest to follow recipe writing styles around. *Pantry Raid's* recipes are straightforward, spare—no unnecessary detail or fussy steps. The whole picture and nothing but the picture. And what appeals to me is the energy. By golly, the prose implies, trust me that this is a great recipe. Let's just get to the kitchen and you'll soon be sitting down to a fabulous dinner.

Now I suspect that Dana McCauley's pantry is pretty well-stocked with ingredients from around the world, and no one uses them with more flair than Ms. McCauley. But to start out, pick just one of the pantries—the Asian one, for example. Then, Dana advises, if you buy a bottle of sesame oil, you'll get to drizzle it into marinades and sauces often. Let that pantry be the building blocks for more.

But enough! *Pantry Raid* is an inspired addition to cookbooks people can keep on their kitchen shelf and turn to for great flavors, delivered with ease.

— Elizabeth Baird

Food Editor of *Canadian Living* magazine and co-host of *Canadian Living Cooks* on Food Network Canada

Introduction

I don't know what happens in your neighborhood, but on my street the pizza delivery man can be seen making the rounds most weeknights at about 6:30 p.m. On Tuesdays and Thursdays he stops two doors down. Mondays I see him across the street and, until I started stocking a more functional pantry myself, most Fridays I used to see him up close at my own front door. Although it turns out he's quite a nice guy, take-out pizza isn't a very satisfying dinner experience.

Although we all blame the demands of our hectic urban and suburban lives for turning evening meal time into crunch time, modern households have never been better equipped for turning out delicious, quickly prepared meals. State of the art appliances, designer gadgets and access to myriad wonderful fresh and semi-prepared ingredients are all at our fingertips waiting to be used to make a yummy dinner. So, truth be told, the only challenges we face are having the right ingredients in the house to make a decent meal and having the cooking skills to prepare simple recipes under a certain amount of time pressure.

Between the covers of *Pantry Raid* you'll find all you need to rise to such challenges. Pantry cooking is here for you! Shopping lists and substitution charts found in the Introduction take care of the organizational dilemmas surrounding weeknight cooking. The following chapters, featuring more than 200 recipes with easy-to-follow directions and icons that highlight the benefits of each recipe, will guide you through meal preparation.

If the mention of "pantry" makes you nervous, relax. I don't expect you to slave over a hot canning kettle. Pantry stocking methods have evolved since our grandmothers spent all summer putting up pickles, tomatoes and preserves. A strategic trip to a well-stocked grocery store for items that can be easily combined to make simple but delicious meals creates today's functional pantries. Plus, nothing *a la king* need come of this exercise. In fact, if you follow my lead you'll easily earn the moniker of gourmet.

Pointers for pantry cooking success

Speed pantry basics: Items like couscous, frozen or canned beans, canned lentils and even frozen french fries can make the difference between being able to pull together a tasty supper quickly or buying dinner ready-made. Among the items you'll need to add dash and zip to quick meals and leftovers are condiments. Stock the larder with a variety of vinegars, chutneys, mustards and bottled sauces. Such products can be used as culinary shortcuts in the kitchen or at the table to boost flavor.

Frozen assets: If you have a microwave with a defrosting mode, the freezer can be a handy pantry-cooking tool. Buy and freeze a selection of small cuts of meat such as chicken stir-fry strips, pork tenderloin, ground meat, steaks, chops and sausages that can be quickly and easily defrosted for use on a weeknight. Be careful to choose packages labeled as *tender cuts*, *fast fry* and *stir-fry* since these meats will still be tender after being cooked quickly. Likewise, if you feel flustered when you have to pull together a basting sauce or marinade, butcher-marinated meats can be turned into tasty dinners.

Leftover luxury: Home-meal-replacements (HMRs) are fresh store-made entrées that are generally expensive when compared to homemade fare. To save money but still have the convenience of an HMR, make double batches of stews, roasts and casseroles on the weekend then hold over a portion for a weeknight supper. This also works with mealtime cornerstones such as grilled or broiled meats, potatoes, rice or pasta; prepare double the amount you need and use half in a skillet supper or hearty salad later in the week.

Herbal magic: Fresh herbs such as basil and coriander perish quickly in the refrigerator but can be finely chopped and frozen in ice cube trays. Once frozen, transfer cubes to freezer bags. Then, when you need a little fresh herb flavor, toss a cube or two into your saucepan.

Helping hands: The advantages of faster preparation and less mess make partially prepared convenience products very attractive for weeknight use. Items such as peeled garlic, bagged and cleaned lettuce, deli-made chicken broth and Break-Free liquid eggs eliminate a few of the temporal roadblocks one often faces when cooking on a weeknight. The cost for such items may be a little higher, but the convenience outweighs the added cost for many busy people.

Make a list: The most important preparation for being able to pull meals out of the cupboard quickly is to have a well-stocked pantry in the first place. That means knowing what to shop for and when you need to buy more. Keep a running list (see page 22 for a template) in a handy place so that when you're off to the store or to the computer to place a grocery order you'll be well organized.

Avoiding the giant: The trend toward bigger grocery stores means one-stop shopping is more convenient. However, picking up a few necessary items at a large store can take longer than it did when stores were smaller. To keep your pantry primed for fast meal preparation, break your grocery shopping trips into monthly, weekly and occasional shopping trips for fresh items. See the checklists below for a list of what to buy when.

Divide and conquer: Once you get the food into the house, you need to be able to find what you need quickly so that foraging through the cupboards doesn't slow you down. One thing you can do is group spices and the like by type of cuisine. For instance, group the fish sauce, hoisin, mirin and sesame oil in one area or a bin so that Asian items are together. Likewise, oregano, tomato paste, pesto, balsamic vinegar, pine nuts and olive oil are common culinary companions so stacking them together means the ingredients for Italian dishes will be at your fingertips.

Shopping strategies

Grocery shopping is a necessary, but time-consuming, task that has to be done before you can start cooking. Even shopping on-line takes time out of your day. To make shopping as easy as possible I've developed the following checklists. After you've consulted the pantry lists on pages 18 to 21 help you hone in on the items that most appeal to your tastes, use these checklists to assess what you need to buy on your next trip to the store.

Once-a-month staples checklist

Ingredient	Average shelf-life
Freezer	
Frozen orange concentrate	1 year
Canned or frozen beans	1 year
Frozen french fries, hash browns, etc.	6 months
Frozen fish, shellfish, meats and veggie burgers, etc.	Fish = 6 months Meat = 10 to 12 months
Frozen pizza dough or bases, tortillas, piecrust and puff pastry	1 month
Frozen peas, corn, spinach and vegetable blends	1 year
Refrigerator	
Shredded and whole pieces of firm cheese	Several months
Break-Free liquid eggs	4 weeks
Anchovy, pesto, wasabi and sun-dried tomato paste	3 months
Mayonnaise and salad dressings	Opened: 2 months Unopened: 8 months
Sesame and nut oils	3 months

Ingredient	Average shelf-life
Cupboard	
Canned tomatoes: diced, stewed, crushed	1 year
Barbecue, curry and other cooking and basting sauces	9 months
Canned soup and broth	1 year
Raisins, dried cranberries and dried apricots	1 year
Balsamic and other vinegars	Several years although flavors diminish once opened
Pickles, capers and marinated artichokes	Opened: 6 months Unopened: 1 to 2 years
Vegetable and olive oils	1 year
Ketchup, mustard and other condiments	6 months
Dried herbs and spices (whenever possible avoid ground herbs)	Indefinitely although flavors diminish quickly once opened
Curry pastes: Indian and Thai	1 year
Canned legumes	1 year
Cans or cubes of vegetable/chicken broth/bouillon	Several years
Hoisin, fish sauce, soy sauce	1 year
Canned fish: tuna, salmon, clams	1 year
Pasta sauce and salsa	1 year
Pasta, noodles, rice, couscous	1 to 2 years

Weekly shopping checklist

Ingredient	Average shelf-life
Sturdy vegetables such as potatoes, carrots, onions, celery, cabbage, etc.	5 to 10 days
Eggs in the shell	2 weeks
Fresh meats	3 to 5 days
Cold cuts	1 week
Soft cheeses such as cream, ricotta and cottage	1 week
Milk, yogurt, sour cream	1 week
Sturdy herbs such as rosemary and thyme	1 week
Bagged lettuce	3 to 5 days
Butter/margarine	2 weeks if refrigerated
Tofu	3 to 5 days
Fresh bread, buns, bagels	1 to 3 days

Superhero substitutes and equivalents

This chart just might save the day sometime when you think you have what you need for a specific recipe in the house but find out that one of the containers is empty. Also, many products are sold in different formats so some essential equivalents are included here to help you, too.

Ingredient	Measurement	Equivalent/substitute
Butter	1 lb (454 g)	2 cups (500 mL)
Buttermilk	1 cup (250 mL)	1 tbsp (15 mL) lemon juice or white vinegar topped up with enough milk to make 1 cup (250 mL). Let stand 10 minutes.
Chocolate	1 square	1 oz (28 g) or 3 tbsp (45 mL) cocoa plus 1 tbsp (15 mL) butter or margarine
Cornstarch	1 tbsp (15 mL)	2 tbsp (30 mL) all-purpose flour
Cream cheese	8 oz (250 g)	1 cup (250 mL)
Curry paste	1 tsp (5 mL)	1/2 tsp (1 mL) curry powder
Dried beans or lentils	1 cup (250 mL)	2 1/4 cups (300 mL) cooked
Fresh bread crumbs	1 cup (250 mL)	2 slices
Granulated sugar	1 cup (250 mL)	1 cup (250 mL) packed brown sugar or 2 cups (500 mL) icing sugar
Hard cheese (cheddar, Swiss, etc.)	1 lb (454 g)	4 cups (1 L) shreds
Light cream	1 cup (250 mL)	2 tbsp (30 mL) butter topped up with enough milk to make 1 cup (250 mL)
Liquid eggs	1/4 cup (50 mL)	1 egg in the shell
Long grain rice	1 cup (250 mL)	3 cups (750 mL) cooked
Tomato sauce	2 cups (500 mL)	3/4 cup (175 mL) tomato paste and 1 cup (250 mL) water

Pantry partners

Not everyone is an omnivore like me. In fact, it's perfectly normal to have favorite flavors and cuisines. So, use the following lists to create a personal pantry that suits your own taste.

Mexican

Barbecue sauce

Black beans

Chili powder

Cilantro

Corn

Cumin

Fresh coriander

Jalapeno and chipotle peppers

Limes

Monterey Jack cheese

Oregano

Refried beans

Salsa

Tomatoes

Tortillas/wraps

Mediterranean

Anchovy paste

Arborio rice

Balsamic vinegar

Basil

Clam juice

Cornmeal

Dried mushrooms

Garlic

Olive oils

Olives

Oregano

Goat cheese, mozzarella, Parmesan, pecorino, provolone

Pasta

Pasta sauce

Pesto

Pine nuts

Red wine vinegar

Romano and garbanzo beans

Rosemary

Saffron

Sun-dried tomatoes

Asian

Chili-garlic sauce/sambal oelek

Cilantro

Coconut milk

Fish sauce

Fresh coriander

Gari (pickled ginger)

Garlic

Ginger

Green and red curry pastes

Hoisin sauce

Honey

Limes and lemons

Mirin

Nori

Oyster sauce

Plum sauce

Rice

Rice and soba noodles

Rice vinegar

Sesame seeds

Soy sauce

Toasted sesame oil

Wasabi

North American

Apple juice

Apple sauce

Butter/margarine

Canned salmon

Canned tomatoes

Canned tuna

Cider vinegar

Dried and frozen cranberries

Horseradish

Ketchup

Long grain rice

Macaroni

Maple syrup

Marmalade

Mayonnaise

Onions

Orange juice

Peanut butter

Steak sauce

Tomato sauce

Vegetable oil

Yellow mustard

Indian

Basmati Rice

Cardamom

Cauliflower

Cayenne

Chutney

Cilantro

Coconut milk

Coriander

Cumin

Curry paste/powder

Fennel seeds

Frozen peas

Lentils

Limes

Onions

Pappadams

Potatoes

Turmeric

Yogurt

French

Butter

Capers

Cheese: brie, goat, Roquefort

Cream

Dijon mustard

Green peppercorns

Herbes de Provence

Mushrooms

Nutmeg

Olive oil

Onions

Sherry vinegar

Tarragon

Thyme

Tomatoes

Middle Eastern

Cayenne

Chickpeas

Cinnamon

Coriander seed

Couscous

Cucumbers

Cumin

Dried apricots

Dried dates

Eggplant

Garlic

Lemons

Olive oil

Raisins

Yogurt

Nibblers

Cheeses

Chocolate

Crackers

Dried fruit, such as: apricots, cranberries, dates, figs, raisins

Dry cereals

Edamame (immature green soybeans in or out of the pod)

Frozen french fries

Green pumpkin seeds

Marshmallows

Nuts

Olives

Pickles

Roasted red peppers

Smoked oysters

Sour cream

Tortillas

Be a power shopper!

Once you've assessed your needs, it's time to make a shopping list. Although I often jot a few things on a scrap piece of paper, the most successful shopping trips occur when I make a plan-of-attack that breaks down the items I need, based on the aisles and sections of the store.

Here's a template to get you started. Feel free to photocopy it so that you can have it handy each time you shop:

Store perimeter	Aisles
Produce:	Sauces, dressings and spreads
Deli counter: Cheese	Canned fruit, vegetables and juice
Meat:	Snacks and sundries

Bakery: Packaged breads Fresh items	Rice, pasta and legumes
Butcher's counter:	Baking, spices and dried herbs
Frozen:	Cereals, cookies, crackers
Dairy: Eggs Cheese Butter and spreads Milk and related products	Cleaning supplies, food wrap, etc.

Maximizing your frozen assets

Having good quality frozen foods on hand can ease meal-planning pressures—especially for working parents and families with a mix of dietary preferences. But ask anyone who owns a chest-style freezer and you'll hear tales of how these appliances can become black holes filled with unidentifiable packages of mystery meat and tasteless clumps of fruit cloaked in ice crystals. To avoid such confusion and to curtail waste, follow these tips for functional freezing.

1. Quality first: It's crucial to start off with high-quality food. Freezing will never improve poor-quality food. So, choose produce that is at its peak then process it, package it and freeze it quickly to maintain maximum flavor, texture and nutrient content.

2. The right stuff: Choose appropriate storage containers for freezing. Bread bags, wax paper, thin plastic wrap and flimsy deli containers are not recommended for freezer use because they let in too much oxygen. Better choices are rigid plastic containers with tight-fitting lids, straight-sided canning jars, heavy-duty zip-top bags, heavy-duty foil paired with heavy-duty plastic wrap or any other item with a low moisture transmission rate.

3. Snug fit: Pack items to be frozen snugly into appropriate containers. If using lidded containers, leave a 1/2-inch (1-cm) headspace to allow for expansion. Otherwise, airtight is the rule since excess air inside the container can

result in freezer burn (a slow patchy drying of food as surface moisture vaporizes in the cold) which causes detrimental changes in texture, nutrient content and taste.

4. The great divide: Separate large batches into usable sizes for your family so you can avoid opening and closing freezer containers frequently.

5. Label everything: Trust me on this one. I grew up living with a mother who never labeled, but who loved to use her freezer. Despite her best intentions she never remembered what was in each package. The result was a series of wacky culinary episodes that saw her make pies out of perogi dough (dental disaster!) and desserts out of beets (okay, so they do look a little like raspberries when frozen). Find a pen and make labels for each package to be frozen before your kid grows up and tells the world about your freezing mishaps. Also note the quantity and the date frozen on each label.

6. Keep cool, baby: The quality of frozen foods suffers if the food is not kept solidly frozen. Ideally the temperature in your freezer should consistently be below 0°F (-18°C). To maintain temperature don't open the door more frequently than necessary and never leave it ajar for more than a few moments. Likewise, add items to the freezer in small batches so that the internal temperature doesn't increase because too many warm items are being introduced at one time.

7. In a flash: Freezing fruits and vegetables quickly at as low a temperature as possible minimizes ice crystal formation that can damage foods and makes them lose moisture when thawed. So, spread items such as berries, sliced fruits or blanched, barely moist vegetables in a single layer on wax paper-lined trays and freeze for 20 to 30 minutes. Once frozen, quickly transfer to labeled freezer containers and return to the freezer. Not only will the textures of foods frozen this way be better, but removing small portions will be possible too.

8. Blanch 'em: This simple technique is essential when freezing most vegetables. Blanching means boiling foods in water for a specific number of minutes. This technique stops the action of enzymes that could continue to change the color of vegetables and it helps to retain vitamins. Prompt cooling in lots of cold water (a technique chefs call "refreshing") ensures crispness. Drain blanched, cooled foods well so that excess moisture doesn't form large ice crystals.

9. Sugar coating: Many old-school freezing mavens recommend tossing fruits to be frozen with granulated sugar or packing them in a sugar syrup. Although this is a good way to hold the color and accentuate the flavor of fruit, it is certainly not mandatory. If using syrup, a 40% syrup, made by boiling 3 cups/750 mL of granulated sugar with 4 cups/1 L of water is recommended.

10. I.D. check: When selecting produce to freeze remember that fully ripe, mature fruit is best. Vegetables are best if slightly immature since they contain less of the sugar that is converted to starch as the vegetable matures.

11. Be exclusive: Although many produce items can be frozen, some are better enjoyed in season or purchased fresh from the grocery store. In my experience, such items include grapes, potatoes, melons and zucchini. For other foods, use the guidelines in this chart to freeze seasonal produce for use all year long. Remember, frozen fruits and vegetables should be used within 12 months, except corn which should be used within 8 months.

Product Vegetables	Pre-freezing Preparation	Tips
Asparagus	Trim and blanch for 2 to 4 minutes depending on thickness.	Alternate tips and ends in packages to get a tight fit.
Beans (wax or green)	Blanch for 3 minutes.	
Beets	Wash, boil for 15 minutes then peel and remove roots and stems.	Freeze only whole, sliced or diced baby beets since larger beets lose texture and flavor when frozen.
Broccoli	Blanch florets for 3 minutes. Drain well before freezing.	Pack heads and stems alternately to ensure a tight fit.
Carrots	Blanch whole baby carrots for 5 minutes and diced or sliced carrots for 3 minutes.	
Cauliflower	If fresh from the field, soak in salted water for $1/2$ hour to remove insects. Blanch florets for 3 minutes.	
Corn kernels	Blanch ears for 4 minutes. Cut kernels from cob.	Flash freeze for easy use later.
Corn on the cob	Blanch for 7 minutes.	Recommend wrapping each ear individually then grouping them together in plastic storage bags. Do not defrost. Instead, boil from frozen for 15 minutes.
Eggplant	Blanch for 4 minutes in acidulated water ($1/2$ cup/125 mL vinegar to each liter of water).	Pat each piece or slice dry and freeze between pieces of plastic wrap.
Herbs	No need to blanch. Just wash and spin dry.	Place chopped herbs in ice cube trays then transfer to zip-top bags when frozen.
Peas	Shell and blanch for $1 1/2$ minutes.	Best flash frozen.
Peppers (sweet or hot)	No need to blanch. Merely quarter, remove seeds and ribs then freeze.	
Tomatoes	Remove hulls and flash freeze.	Only good for cooked dishes once frozen. Skins slip off when melting.

Product	Pre-freezing Preparation	Tips
Fruits		
Apples	Wash, peel, core and slice.	Dip in acidulated water (see eggplant) or toss with fruit fresh to prevent browning.
Berries	Hull if necessary. Wash gently and pat dry.	Flash freeze for best results.
Cherries	Stem and pit.	Flash freeze for best results. Freezing with pit can produce bitterness.
Cranberries	Freeze in bags they are sold in.	
Peaches/nectarines	Blanch for 30 seconds. Remove skin and pit then slice.	Dip in acidulated water (see eggplant) or toss with fruit fresh.
Pears	Wash, peel, core and halve or slice.	Dip in acidulated water (see eggplant) or toss with fruit fresh.
Plums	Sort, wash and pit. Blanch only if you want to remove the skin.	
Rhubarb	Wash and cut off both ends. Cut into 1-inch (2.5-cm) lengths.	
Meat and poultry		
Small cuts of meat	Wrap tightly in 2 layers of heavy-duty plastic wrap. Defrost in plastic wrap overnight on a plate on the lower rack of refrigerator.	
Large cuts of meat and poultry	Wrap tightly in 2 layers of heavy-duty plastic wrap. Defrost in plastic wrap overnight or over several days on a plate on the lower rack of refrigerator.	
Fish and seafood		
Fish fillets and shrimp	Wrap tightly in 2 layers of heavy-duty plastic wrap. Defrost shrimp by running under cold water until ice crystals disappear. Defrost other shellfish and fish fillets overnight on a plate on the lower rack of refrigerator.	

One would assume...

When using this book you should know that while develop-
ing recipes I make the following assumptions:

Milk is 2% unless otherwise noted

Butter is salted

Eggs are large

The size of fruits and vegetables is average or medium
unless otherwise noted

Produce is washed and dried before you start cooking

Garlic is always peeled

Unless specified, shrimp are raw

Green onions have roots and straggly tips removed

Peppers have white membranes, seeds and stems
removed

Fresh herbs should be removed from the stem before
chopping unless otherwise noted

Pepper is always freshly ground

Decoding the icons

Next to each recipe name you'll find an icon or set of icons that will help you to find quickly recipes that suit your cooking needs. Use this legend to decode the icons.

family favorite

fast but fancy

fast fix

healthier choice

leftover wizard

light

make-ahead

meatless

pantry plus

pantry trick

Starters and Snacks

Warm Goat Cheese Spread

fast but fancy

pantry plus

make-ahead

This sophisticated appetizer is easy to make and it keeps well once assembled. Serve with crunchy, cold grapes and Melba rounds.

¼ cup (50 mL)	chopped sun-dried tomatoes packed in oil
1	clove garlic, minced
1 tsp (5 mL)	grated lemon peel
2 tbsp (30 mL)	chopped fresh dill
2 rolls (4oz/100 g each)	creamy chèvre-style goat cheese
¼ cup (50 mL)	finely chopped toasted cashews

Combine sun-dried tomatoes, garlic, lemon peel and dill in a blender or mini-chopper. Purée until almost smooth. Add the goat cheese and pulse until combined. Scrape goat cheese mixture onto a large piece of plastic wrap. Using the wrap as a guide, shape the goat cheese into a ball. Refrigerate until ready to heat. (Can be prepared to this point and refrigerated for up to 4 days.)

Preheat oven to 375°F (190°C). Spread the chopped cashews on a plate. Unwrap the goat cheese and press into the nuts until evenly encrusted. Place on a pie plate and bake for 12 to 15 minutes or until heated through. Slide a metal spatula under cheese and transfer to a platter. Serve with crudités, Melba rounds and grapes.

Makes 10 servings

Tip: Store toasted cashews at room temperature in a zip-top bag, if preparing ahead.

fast but fancy

make-ahead

meatless

Caramelized Onion and Cheese Dipping Loaf

Prized for its flavor, appeal and portability, this appetizer is ideal for entertaining or for potluck parties.

1	round loaf sourdough bread
1 8 oz (250 g) pkg	brick-style cream cheese, softened
8 oz (250 g)	brie, cubed with rind left intact
	Sublimely Delicious Caramelized Onions (page 165)

Cut a large circle in the top of the loaf. Remove crust in one piece and slice off any jagged bits of bread to make a lid. Scoop bread out of loaf, leaving about a 1-inch (5-cm) layer around the inside. Reserve bread pieces for dipping.

Cream the cheeses together and stir in the onion mixture. Scrape into hollowed loaf. Cover with bread lid. (Can be made up to 3 days ahead, wrapped and refrigerated or up to 2 weeks ahead, wrapped and frozen. Bring to room temperature before baking.)

Preheat oven to 325°F (160°C). Bake loaf for 25 to 35 minutes or until outside is toasted and cheese mixture is warm and soft. Cut lid into bite-size pieces and serve with reserved bread or crudités.

Makes 8 servings.

Curried Cheese Ball

Another party trick that can be pulled off in a heartbeat.

2 8 oz (250 g) pkg	brick-style cream cheese, softened
2 tbsp (30 mL)	mild Indian curry paste
1 tbsp (15 mL)	lime or lemon juice
1 tsp (5 mL)	dry mustard
1	green onion, finely chopped
2 tbsp (30 mL)	smooth mango chutney
1 cup (250 mL)	toasted pecan halves or sliced almonds

Cut cream cheese into chunks and cream with the back of a spoon. Work in curry paste, citrus juice, dry mustard and green onions until well combined. Turn onto plastic wrap and shape into a ball. Chill until firm, about 30 minutes. (Can be made to this point and stored in the refrigerator for up to 3 days.)

Spread top and sides of cheese ball with chutney. Coat outside evenly with nuts. Serve with crackers, naan bread or crudités.

Makes 10 to 12 servings.

pantry trick

fast fix

Dip-it-ee-do-da!

If you have 1 cup (250 mL) sour cream, you can create an instant dip for veggies, bread, chips, crackers or even chicken fingers from things you have on hand.

Pesto: Stir 2 tbsp (30 mL) basil pesto into sour cream. Add salt and pepper to taste.

Curry: Stir 1 tsp (5 mL) mild curry paste or 1½ tsp (7 mL) curry powder and 2 tbsp (30 mL) finely chopped chives into sour cream. Add salt and pepper to taste.

Southwest chicken finger dip: Stir 1 tsp (5 mL) chili powder and 2 tbsp (30 mL) barbecue sauce into sour cream.

Double dill pickle: Stir 2 tsp (10 mL) dillweed and ¼ cup (50 mL) finely diced dill pickles into sour cream. Add salt and pepper to taste.

Chutney: Stir 2 tbsp (30 mL) each mango chutney and finely chopped fresh mint and ½ tsp (2 mL) ground cumin into sour cream. Add salt and pepper to taste.

Lemon-tarragon: Stir 1 tsp (5 mL) each finely grated lemon peel and chopped fresh tarragon into sour cream. Add salt and pepper to taste.

Tangy balsamic-tomato: Stir 2 tbsp (30 mL) sun-dried (or regular) tomato paste and 2 tsp (10 mL) balsamic vinegar into sour cream. Add 2 tbsp (30 mL) chopped fresh basil, if you like. Add salt and pepper to taste.

Thai flavors: Stir 2 tsp (10 mL) red or green Thai curry paste into sour cream.

Smoked salmon and dill: Combine ¼ cup (50 mL) finely chopped smoked salmon, 1 tbsp (15 mL) fresh dill and 1 tsp (5 mL) chopped capers with sour cream in a blender or food processor. Blend until almost smooth. Add ½ tsp (2 mL) finely grated lemon peel if you like. Add salt and pepper to taste.

Savory Tofu Spread

This spread can be flavored as you like (see the mayonnaise variations on page 63 for ideas).

1 box (300 g)	soft or silken tofu
1/4 cup (50 mL)	olive oil
1 1/2 tsp (7 mL)	Dijon mustard
1 tbsp (15 mL)	lemon juice or cider vinegar
2 tbsp (30 mL)	chopped fresh parsley
1 tbsp (15 mL)	chopped fresh basil or thyme
1/2 tsp (2 mL)	salt and pepper

Combine the tofu with the oil in a food processor. Purée until smooth. Scrape down the sides. Add the mustard, lemon juice or vinegar, parsley and basil or thyme and blend until smooth. Add salt and pepper. Scrape into a bowl and refrigerate until ready to use.

Variation:

Tofu hummus: Substitute firm tofu for silken and add 1 minced garlic clove. Blend until almost smooth.

meatless

fast fix

pantry trick

pantry plus

fast but fancy

meatless

Sushi Stack Canapés

Assemble this simplified sushi just before serving so that the base doesn't become soggy.

1 cup (250 mL)	#1 grade sushi or short grain rice
1¼ cups (300 mL)	water
2 tbsp (30 mL)	rice vinegar
1 tbsp (15 mL)	granulated sugar
1 tsp (5 mL)	salt
5	sheets nori (dried edible seaweed)

Toppings:

4 oz (125 g)	thinly sliced smoked salmon or very fresh center-cut raw tuna or salmon
	flying fish roe
	pickled ginger
	wasabi paste
	soy sauce

Place rice in a large, heavy saucepan and add water, vinegar, sugar and salt. Cover and place over medium-high heat until water comes to a boil. Reduce heat to low and boil (without peeking under lid) for 15 minutes. Remove from heat and let stand for 10 minutes. Remove lid and transfer rice to a tray or platter.

Spread rice out on a cookie sheet and let cool to room temperature. Do not refrigerate. (Rice can be made up to 4 hours ahead then covered with a clean, damp towel and stored at room temperature until needed.)

Cut each sheet of nori into 16 squares, using kitchen scissors. Place a spoonful of rice on top of each square. Top with thinly sliced fish and fish roe or topping choices of your own. Serve immediately with pickled ginger, wasabi paste and soy sauce for dipping on the side.

Makes 80 canapés.

Vegetarian Variations:

Carrot and avocado: Substitute shredded carrot and sliced avocado for fish.

Green mango and green onion: Substitute shredded green mango and sliced green onion for fish.

Asian Glazed Pork Rolls

Although they look difficult to make, these appetizers are a breeze to prepare.

1/2 lb. (250 g)	pork tenderloin
5	green onions
1/2	red pepper
1/4 cup (50 mL)	plum sauce
1/4 cup (50 mL)	hoisin sauce
2 tbsp (30 mL)	soy sauce
2 tbsp (30 mL)	liquid honey
2 tsp (10 mL)	sesame oil
2 tsp (10 mL)	minced ginger root
1/2 tsp (2 mL)	sambal oelek or hot pepper sauce

Trim any fat from pork and wrap tightly in plastic wrap; place in freezer for 45 minutes or until firm but not solid. Cut onions and red peppers into 2-inch (5-cm) lengths; reserve. Stir together plum, hoisin, soy sauce, honey, sesame oil, ginger and sambal oelek or hot sauce.

Slice partially frozen pork as thinly as possible into medallions. Using the side of a chef's knife or a mallet, flatten meat until very thin. Brush surface lightly with sauce and tightly roll each slice around either a piece of green onion or red pepper strip.

Brush sauce liberally all over finished rolls and place on a lightly greased, foil-lined, rimmed baking sheet. (Rolls can be made to this point up to 4 hours ahead, wrapped and refrigerated; bring to room temperature for 30 minutes before cooking.)

Preheat oven to 400°F (220°C). Bake for 10 minutes, brushing frequently with remaining sauce until rolls are well glazed. Brush one last time and place under broiler for 2 minutes or until sauce is bubbly.

Makes about 4 dozen rolls.

Salmon Ribbon Satays

Prepare these satays up to 8 hours ahead and then cook them as needed during the party.

¹/₄ cup (50 mL)	hoisin sauce
1 tbsp (15 mL)	lime or lemon juice
1 lb (500 g)	skinless salmon fillet
2 tbsp (30 mL)	thickly sliced chives
	lime wedges
	wooden skewers

Soak 20 wooden skewers in water for 5 minutes. Meanwhile, in a shallow bowl or glass baking dish, stir hoisin with citrus juice. Reserve.

Slice the salmon lengthwise into 20 thin strips and thread each strip onto a skewer. Place in hoisin mixture and turn until coated. Let stand for at least 20 minutes or up to 8 hours in the refrigerator.

Place on a greased broiling pan. Cook, turning once, on a rack set 4 inches (10 cm) below the upper element for 4 to 6 minutes or until caramelized on the outside but still slightly pink inside. Remove from pan and arrange on a platter. Sprinkle with chives and serve with lime wedges on the side.

Makes 20 servings.

Tip: Remove skin from salmon by slipping the tip of a sharp knife under one corner. Grasp flap of skin with the fingers of one hand and pull skin from fish while moving the knife from side to side with the other hand.

pantry plus

fast fix

fast but fancy

Grilled Shrimp Cocktail

Although shrimp cocktail may seem old-fashioned, everyone will enjoy this updated version.

1/3 cup (75 mL)	ketchup
2 tsp (10 mL)	prepared horseradish
1/2 tsp (2 mL)	finely grated lime peel
1 tsp (5 mL)	lime juice
1/4 tsp (1 mL)	Worcestershire sauce
1/4 cup (50 mL)	olive oil
1 tbsp (15 mL)	chopped fresh thyme or 1 tsp (5 mL) dried thyme
1 tbsp (15 mL)	chopped fresh parsley or 1 tsp (5 mL) dried parsley
1/2 tsp (2 mL)	each coarsely ground pepper and salt
1	clove garlic, minced
1 lb (500 g)	jumbo shrimp, cleaned and deveined
	wooden skewers

Soak sixteen 6-inch (18-cm) wooden skewers in warm water. Stir ketchup with horseradish, lime peel and juice and Worcestershire sauce (Can be covered and stored in refrigerator for up to 5 days.)

Stir oil with thyme, parsley, pepper, salt and garlic. Pat shrimp dry and turn in oil mixture until evenly coated. Thread 2 shrimp onto tip of each skewer.

Preheat grill to medium-high. Place skewers on hot grill. Cook, turning once and brushing with remaining oil mixture, for about 5 minutes or until pink and cooked through. Arrange on a platter around bowl of sauce.

Makes 8 servings.

Lime-Coconut Sweet Potato Bites

healthier choice

meatless

Party food isn't always healthy but these morsels are an excellent source of vitamin A and a wise choice for anyone who wants to avoid high fat foods.

2	sweet potatoes, about 2 lbs (1 kg)
2 tbsp (30 mL)	butter
1	small clove garlic, sliced
2 tbsp (30 mL)	toasted desiccated coconut
1 tsp (5 mL)	finely grated lime peel
1 tbsp (15 mL)	lime juice
dash	hot pepper sauce
	salt
	toothpicks

Peel potatoes and cut into 1/2-in (1-cm) cubes. Place in a medium saucepan and cover with cold, salted water. Bring to a boil and simmer until almost fork tender, about 3 minutes. Drain well and pat dry with paper towel.

Melt butter in a skillet set over medium-high heat. Add garlic and cook, stirring, for 1 minute. Remove garlic and discard. When pan is hot, add cubes of potato and cook, turning until golden on each side, about 8 minutes. Add coconut, lime peel, lime juice and hot pepper sauce to pan; toss potatoes to coat evenly. Taste and add salt if necessary.

Skewer each cube with a toothpick and arrange on a platter. Serve at room temperature.

Makes about 3 dozen.

fast fix

pantry trick

Saturday Night Pizza Crisps

If you find the weekends hard to endure without evening snacks, then you need these crisp little bites that can be prepared in just 5 minutes!

4	wheat flour tortillas, each 6 inches (15 cm) wide
1/2 cup (125 mL)	pizza or pasta sauce
1 cup (250 mL)	shredded mozzarella cheese or Italian blend of shredded cheeses
1 cup (250 mL)	sliced mushrooms or diced red or green pepper
2 tbsp (30 mL)	grated Parmesan cheese

Preheat oven to 400°F (200°C). Arrange tortillas in a single layer on baking sheets and place in the oven for 2 minutes. Turn and spread sauce evenly over each tortilla. Sprinkle evenly with cheese, mushrooms or peppers and Parmesan cheese.

Return to oven for 5 minutes or until cheese is bubbly. Transfer to a cutting board and cut each tortilla into 8 wedges.

Makes 8 servings.

Wonton Crisps

healthier choice

pantry trick

fast fix

As satisfying as a crunchy potato chip but fat-free! What could be better when the munchies attack?

10	spring roll wrappers
1 tbsp (15 mL)	tamari or soy sauce
1/4 tsp (1 mL)	hot pepper sauce
2 tsp (10 mL)	sesame seeds

Preheat oven to 350°F (180°C). Cut stack of wrappers into quarters on the diagonal to make 4 stacks of triangles. Peel apart and lay flat on baking sheets. In a small bowl combine tamari or soy sauce and hot pepper sauce.

Brush sauce evenly over tops of triangles. Sprinkle evenly with sesame seeds. Bake in oven for about 4 minutes or until crisp. Cool completely. Serve or store in an airtight container for up to 2 days.

Makes 40 crisps.

Tip: Substitute egg roll wrappers for spring roll wrappers if necessary. Increase cooking time to 8 minutes.

Variations:

Nacho cheese: Omit tamari, hot pepper sauce and sesame seeds. Combine 2 tsp (10 mL) vegetable oil with 1 tsp (5 mL) chili powder and 1/4 tsp (1 mL) each salt and pepper. Sprinkle over wontons and bake as specified above.

Salt and vinegar: Omit tamari, hot pepper sauce and sesame seeds. Brush 1 tbsp (15 mL) white wine vinegar evenly over wontons. Sprinkle with 1/4 to 1/2 tsp (1 to 2 mL) salt and bake as specified above.

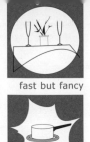

fast but fancy

fast fix

Pangaea Spiced Olives

My husband Martin Kouprie always has a dish of these great olives on the bar at Pangaea, his downtown Toronto restaurant.

1 tbsp (15 mL)	fruity olive oil
2	cloves garlic, thinly sliced
1 tbsp (15 mL)	coarsely chopped fresh rosemary
1 tbsp (15 mL)	dried thyme
1/2 tsp (2 mL)	hot pepper flakes
2 cups (500 mL)	cured large green olives
2 cups (500 mL)	Gaeta or kalamata olives
1 tsp (5 mL)	coarsely grated lemon peel

Warm oil in a large skillet set over medium heat. Add garlic and cook, stirring often, for 3 minutes or until fragrant. Remove garlic and discard. Add rosemary, thyme and hot pepper flakes; cook, stirring often, for 2 minutes. Toss in olives and cook, stirring, for 2 to 3 minutes or until warm. Stir in lemon peel and place in a deep platter or shallow pasta bowl.

Makes 4 cups (1 L).

Macho-Nacho Popcorn

A zesty, easy snack that's great for family video night.

1	bag microwave popping corn, about 8 cups (2 L) popped
4 tsp (20 mL)	butter
1 tsp (5 mL)	chili powder
1/4 tsp (1 mL)	ground cumin
1/4 tsp (1 mL)	each salt and pepper
1 tbsp (15 mL)	grated Parmesan cheese

Place popped popcorn in a clean plastic bag. Place butter in a heatproof bowl and melt in microwave. Stir in chili powder, cumin, salt and pepper. Drizzle into popcorn bag and add Parmesan cheese. Shake to combine.

Makes 8 servings.

healthier choice

pantry trick

Curried Oven–Dried Apple Slices

These crisp savories offer a great way to beat cravings for salty snacks as peanuts and chips.

2 tbsp (30 mL)	lemon juice
2 tbsp (30 mL)	water
2 tsp (10 mL)	mild Indian curry paste
8	Granny Smith apples, cored

Preheat oven to 200°F (95°C). Stir lemon juice with water and curry paste until smooth. Slice cored apples very thinly. Brush apples all over with curry mixture.

Spread apples out in a single layer on baking trays. Bake in oven for 2 to 3 hours, turning occasionally, until crisp and light brown. Cool to room temperature.

Makes 8 servings.

Sushi Stack Canapés, page 38

Asian Glazed Pork Rolls, page 40

Beautiful Beet Borscht, page 52

Grilled Shrimp Cocktail, page 42

Soups, Vegetables and Other Salads

Abracadabra Lentil Soup

High in fiber, folic acid and iron, this fast soup is for anyone who wants to feel and look great but still eat well.

1 tbsp (15 mL)	vegetable oil
1	onion, peeled and chopped
1	clove garlic, minced
1 tsp (5 mL)	ground cumin
1 tsp (5 mL)	finely grated orange peel
1/2 tsp (2 mL)	ground allspice
1/2 tsp (2 mL)	coriander seed
1/2 tsp (2 mL)	pepper
4 cups (1 L)	vegetable or chicken broth
2 cans (19 oz/391 mL each)	cooked brown lentils, or about 3 cups (750 mL) cooked or frozen lentils
1/4 cup (50 mL)	chopped fresh parsley
2 tbsp (30 mL)	plain yogurt

Heat oil in a large saucepan set over medium heat. Add the onion, garlic, cumin, orange peel, allspice, coriander and pepper. Cook, stirring often, for 5 minutes. Add broth and bring to a boil. Rinse lentils and add to pan; return to boil. Simmer for 7 to 10 minutes.

Purée soup, working in batches, in a blender or food processor until smooth, or almost smooth if you prefer a more rustic soup. Return to saucepan and reheat. Stir in parsley and serve with a dollop of yogurt in the center.

Makes 4 to 6 servings.

healthier choice

meatless

make-ahead

Beautiful Beet Borscht

A soup with an ugly name really can be beautiful to behold!

1 tbsp (15 mL)	vegetable oil
1	large onion, peeled and chopped
1	stalk celery, chopped
1	carrot, chopped
1	bay leaf
4	beets with greens
4 cups (1 L)	chicken or vegetable broth
1 can (28 oz/791 mL)	diced tomatoes
1 tbsp (15 mL)	balsamic vinegar
3 tbsp (45 mL)	coarsely chopped fresh dill
1 tsp (5 mL)	finely grated orange peel
1/4 cup (50 mL)	plain yogurt or sour cream

Tip: When working with beets, prevent stained hands by coating skin lightly with petroleum jelly.

Heat oil in a large heavy saucepan set over medium heat. Add the onion, celery, carrot and bay leaf. Cook, stirring often, for 10 minutes or until vegetables are very soft.

Trim stalks from beets. Cut off greens and discard stems or reserve for another use. Wash greens and pat dry. Coarsely shred enough leaves to make 1 cup (250 mL). Reserve.

Use a vegetable peeler or paring knife to peel beets and cut into 1/4-inch (5-cm) cubes. Add beets, broth, tomatoes, including their juices, and vinegar to the saucepan. Cover and bring to a boil. Reduce heat and simmer for 35 to 40 minutes or until beets are tender.

Stir in greens. Cook for 2 minutes. Stir in dill and orange peel. Taste and adjust seasoning if needed. Discard bay leaf. Serve soup hot or chilled with a dollop of yogurt.

Makes 6 servings.

Hot 'n' Sour Scallop Soup

meatless

fast but fancy

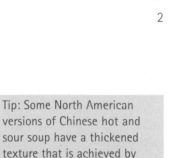

fast fix

Quickly prepared, satisfying and healthy too!

6 cups (1.5 L)	vegetable or chicken broth
1	dried wood ear mushroom
4 tsp (20 mL)	minced ginger root
1 tbsp (15 mL)	rice vinegar
1 tsp (5 mL)	granulated sugar
1 tsp (5 mL)	sambal oelek or hot pepper sauce
3 tbsp (45 mL)	tamari or soy sauce
1 tsp (5 mL)	toasted sesame oil
4 oz (125 g)	silken or soft tofu
8 oz (250 g)	bay scallops, muscle removed
2	green onions, sliced

Tip: Some North American versions of Chinese hot and sour soup have a thickened texture that is achieved by whisking cornstarch into the stock mixture. If you miss this texture, whisk 1 to 2 tbsp (15 to 30 mL) of cornstarch into broth and simmer for 2 minutes before adding mushrooms, scallops and green onion.

Heat 1 cup (250 mL) of broth and pour over wood ear mushroom; let mushroom soak for about 10 minutes or until softened. Drain, reserving broth, and slice mushroom as thinly as possible. Reserve.

Combine remaining broth with ginger, vinegar, sugar, sambal oelek or hot sauce, tamari or soy sauce, and sesame oil in saucepan set over medium-high heat. Bring to boil. Taste and adjust seasoning if necessary.

Drain and dice tofu into tiny cubes. Stir scallops, reserved mushroom, soaking liquid, tofu and green onions into soup. Cook for 1 minute or until piping hot.

Makes 6 servings.

pantry trick

family favorite

Fifteen-Minute Chinese Chicken Noodle Soup

Using common pantry and freezer basics, this hearty spoon-and-fork style soup is a meal in a bowl that delivers important nutrients such as B vitamins and iron.

4 cups (1 L)	chicken broth
1 tsp (5 mL)	minced ginger root
1	clove garlic, minced
2 tbsp (30 mL)	light or medium soy sauce
1	fine egg noodle nest
1 cup (250 mL)	chopped, leftover cooked chicken (optional)
1 1/2 cups (375 mL)	frozen Asian-style vegetable blend
2	green onions, sliced on the diagonal
	nori (optional)

Bring chicken broth to a boil in a deep sacuepan set over medium-high heat. Add ginger, garlic and soy sauce and return to boil. Drop in noodles and stir until they are no longer clumped. Boil for 5 minutes. Add chicken.

Place vegetables in a colander and run under cold running water until all the ice crystals are removed. Drain well. Add to soup and bring to a boil. Stir in green onions. Crumble over a little nori if you like.

Makes 2 to 3 servings.

Tip: Substitute leftover steamed or stir-fried vegetables for frozen.

Moroccan Chunky Tomato Soup

This mixture can be used as a soup or pasta sauce.

1 tbsp (15 mL)	olive or other vegetable oil
1	onion, peeled and chopped
1 tsp (5 mL)	grated orange peel
1/2 tsp (2 mL)	ground cumin
1/4 tsp (1 mL)	ground cinnamon
pinch	cayenne
2 cans (28 oz/791 mL each)	diced tomatoes
1/4 cup (50 mL)	chopped fresh parsley or basil (optional)

Heat oil in a saucepan set over medium heat. Add onion, orange peel, cumin, cinnamon and cayenne. Cook, stirring often, for 7 to 10 minutes or until onion is soft. Stir in tomatoes and bring to a boil. Simmer for 5 minutes. Stir in parsley or basil (if using). Serve hot, or chill approximately 2 hours and serve cold.

Makes 6 servings.

Tip: Taste and add up to 1/2 tsp (2 mL) granulated sugar or balsamic vinegar depending on whether soup is too tart or too sweet.

pantry trick

meatless

make-ahead

fast but fancy

meatless

Cream of Fresh Tomato Soup with a Pesto Swirl

A favorite childhood recipe grows up.

1 tbsp (15 mL)	butter
1	onion, peeled, halved and thinly sliced
1	clove garlic, minced
2 cans (28 oz/791 mL each)	tomato purée, about 6 cups (1.5 L)
1½ tsp (7 mL)	salt
½ tsp (2 mL)	white pepper
1 cup (250 mL)	35% whipping cream, half-and-half or homogenized milk
2 tbsp (30 mL)	basil pesto

Melt butter in a large saucepan set over medium heat. Add the onion and garlic. Cook, stirring often, for 5 minutes. Add to softened onion. Stir while bringing to a boil.

Reduce the heat to low. Cover and simmer for 20 minutes, stirring occasionally. Pass though a fine mesh sieve and return to pan. Stir in salt, pepper and cream. Heat until steaming.

Serve warm or chilled. Add 1 tsp (5 mL) of pesto to each bowl. Swirl with the tip of a knife to make a pattern, if you like.

Makes 6 servings.

Sweet Potato Coconut Soup

fast but fancy

leftover wizard

This velvety smooth soup, bursting with vitamin A, tastes so rich and satisfying that it's hard to imagine it could be so easy to make!

1 tbsp (15 mL)	vegetable oil
1	small onion, peeled and chopped
1/2 tsp (2 mL)	mild Indian curry paste
1 lb (500 g)	peeled sweet potatoes, about 3 cups (750 mL)
1	clove garlic, chopped
3 cups (750 mL)	chicken or vegetable broth
1 cup (250 mL)	coconut milk
1	lime
2 tbsp (30 mL)	chopped fresh coriander
1/2 tsp (2 mL)	each salt and pepper

Heat oil in a medium saucepan set over medium heat. Add onion and curry paste and cook, stirring often, for 5 minutes. Meanwhile, chop sweet potatoes into small pieces. Add sweet potatoes and garlic to saucepan and cook, stirring often, for 10 minutes or until potatoes are slightly softened. Stir in broth and bring to a boil. Reduce heat to medium-low and simmer, covered, for 10 to 15 minutes or until potatoes are soft.

Transfer to a blender or food processor and blend, working in batches, until smooth. Return to pan and stir in coconut milk. Using a zester or a hand grater, remove the peel from the lime and chop finely. Add 1 tsp (5 mL) of the peel to the soup. Juice the lime and add 2 tsp (10 mL) juice to the soup. Stir in coriander, salt and pepper to taste.

Makes 2 to 3 servings.

fast but fancy

pantry plus

Cream of Shiitake Soup

Fuller-flavored and more satisfying than its canned cousin, this fast soup is as appropriate for a dinner party menu as it is for the weeknight dinner table.

1 tbsp (15 mL)	vegetable oil
1	small onion, peeled and chopped
4 cups (1 L)	sliced shiitake, button or brown mushrooms
1 tsp (5 mL)	dried thyme leaves
1/4 tsp (1 mL)	finely grated lemon peel (optional)
1/2 tsp (2 mL)	pepper
1/4 tsp (1 mL)	salt
1 tbsp (15 mL)	butter
2 tbsp (30 mL)	all-purpose flour
2 cups (500 mL)	chicken or vegetable broth
2 cups (500 mL)	homogenized milk

Heat the oil in a deep saucepan set over medium heat. Add the onion and cook, stirring occasionally, for 5 minutes. Increase the heat to medium-high and add the mushrooms. Cook, stirring often, for 5 minutes or until browned. Stir in thyme, lemon peel (if using), pepper and salt. Remove from pan. Reserve.

Return saucepan to burner, reduce heat to medium-low. Melt the butter and sprinkle in flour. Stir until lightly browned. Add a splash of broth and stir until smooth. Add remaining broth and milk. Stirring, bring to a boil. Cook, stirring, for 5 minutes or until slightly thickened.

Stir in mushrooms and any accumulated juices. Cook, stirring, for 2 to 3 minutes or until mushrooms are heated through. Taste and adjust seasoning if necessary.

Makes 3 to 4 servings.

Fresh Pea Soup

healthier choice

fast fix

Light-textured and fresh-tasting, this is not at all like the classic split pea soup most people think of when they hear the words "pea soup."

1 tbsp (15 mL)	butter or vegetable oil
1	sliced leek (tender white part only)
1/4 tsp (1 mL)	each salt and pepper
pinch	granulated sugar
2 cups (500 mL)	fresh or frozen baby peas
1 cup (250 mL)	finely shredded romaine lettuce
2 tbsp (30 mL)	chopped fresh parsley
6 cups (1.5 L)	vegetable or chicken broth

Melt butter or heat oil in a large saucepan set over medium heat. Add leek, salt, pepper and sugar. Cook, stirring, for 5 minutes or until softened. Add peas, lettuce, parsley and 1 cup (250 mL) of the broth. Cover and cook over medium heat for 5 minutes or until peas are tender.

Purée soup, working in batches, in blender or food processor until very smooth. Add remaining broth as necessary to make a smooth mixture. Return to pan and stir in broth that hasn't been added. Reheat until mixture boils.

Makes 4 to 6 servings.

fast fix

Why buy expensive salad dressings when they are so easy to pull out of the cupboard?

Cal-Ital Dressing

Great on greens and grilled veggies.

2 tbsp (30 mL)	balsamic vinegar
2 tbsp (30 mL)	pesto
1/2 tsp (2 mL)	dried thyme leaves
1/4 tsp (1 mL)	each salt and pepper
2	oil-packed sun-dried tomatoes, chopped
1/2 cup (125 mL)	extra virgin olive oil

Combine balsamic vinegar with pesto, thyme, salt, pepper and sun-dried tomatoes in a mini-chopper or blender. Chop well. Add olive oil and blend until well combined. Store tightly covered in the refrigerator for up to 1 week.

Makes 3/4 cup (175 mL).

Basic Vinaigrette

This recipe should be like your phone number, one of those things you just know. If you can't remember it, consider having it tattooed on your wrist for easy reference.

1 tbsp (15 mL)	white or red wine vinegar
1/2 tsp (2 mL)	Dijon mustard
1/4 tsp (1 mL)	each salt and pepper
pinch	granulated sugar
1/4 cup (50 mL)	extra virgin olive oil

Stir vinegar, mustard, salt, pepper and sugar until mixed well. Whisking, drizzle in olive oil. Recipe doubles and triples easily.

Makes about 1/3 cup (75 mL).

Variations:

Tuscan sunshine: Substitute balsamic vinegar for wine vinegar and stir in 1/2 tsp (2 mL) finely chopped fresh rosemary and 1/2 tsp (2 mL) finely grated lemon peel.

Orchard: Substitute cider vinegar for wine vinegar and stir in 1/2 tsp (2 mL) chopped fresh thyme.

Red peppercorn: Crush 1/4 tsp (1 mL) red peppercorns and add to vinegar mixture. Increase sugar to 1/2 tsp (2 mL).

Saffron: Soak 1/4 tsp (1 mL) saffron threads in 1 tsp (5 mL) very hot water. Stir into vinegar mixture. Substitute vegetable oil for extra virgin olive oil.

Lemon-lime: Substitute 1 tsp (5 mL) each lemon and lime juice for vinegar. Increase sugar to 1/2 tsp (2 mL).

pantry trick

fast fix

make-ahead

Safe Caesar Dressing

Because this recipe uses pasteurized liquid eggs, you won't have to worry about the health issues associated with classic caesar recipes.

1/4 cup (50 mL)	pasteurized liquid eggs, well shaken
2 tbsp (30 mL)	grated Parmesan cheese
2 tbsp (30 mL)	red wine vinegar
1 tbsp (15 mL)	lemon juice
1 tsp (5 mL)	Dijon mustard
1/2 tsp (2 mL)	Worcestershire sauce
1/2 tsp (2 mL)	anchovy paste
1/4 tsp (1 mL)	pepper
2	small cloves garlic
3/4 cup (175 mL)	extra virgin olive oil
	salt

Combine eggs with Parmesan, vinegar, lemon juice, mustard, Worcestershire sauce, anchovy paste, pepper and garlic in a blender. Blend until well mixed. With motor running, drizzle in olive oil. Taste and add salt to taste.

Use immediately or cover and store in refrigerator for up to 7 days.

Makes approximately 1 cup (250 mL).

Tips: Pasteurized liquid eggs are sold under the brand names such as Omega Pro and Break-Free.

Shake the carton well before measuring out eggs.

Mayo Magic

fast fix

make-ahead

Enjoy the taste of gourmet mayonnaise without the health risks traditionally associated with homemade mayonnaise.

1/4 cup (50 mL)	pasteurized liquid eggs, well shaken
1 tbsp (15 mL)	fresh lemon juice
2 tsp (10 mL)	Dijon mustard
pinch	each salt and white pepper
2/3 cup (150 mL)	vegetable oil

Combine eggs with lemon juice, mustard, salt and pepper in a blender. Mix until combined. Drizzle in oil with motor running. Blend until thick. Keeps in an airtight container in refrigerator for up to 2 weeks.

Makes 1 1/4 cups (300 mL).

Variations:

Roasted garlic: Add 1 tbsp (15 mL) mashed roasted garlic before adding oil.

Indian: Add 3/4 tsp (4 mL) mild Indian curry paste and 1/4 tsp (1 mL) finely grated lime peel before adding oil.

Basil: Add 2 tbsp (30 mL) chopped fresh basil before adding oil.

meatless

fast fix

make-ahead

Nutless Basil Pesto

This is the basic pesto I use in many of the other recipes in this book. You can also use a good quality, store-bought pesto. I recommend the types available in the refrigerator section of specialty supermarkets for the freshest taste.

2^1/$_2$ cups (625 mL)	cleaned, packed fresh basil leaves
1 cup (250 mL)	cleaned, packed fresh parsley leaves
3/4 cup (175 mL)	grated Parmesan cheese
2 tbsp (30 mL)	lemon juice
1/2 tsp (2 mL)	salt
4	cloves garlic (about 4 tsp/20 mL minced)
3/4 cup (175 mL)	extra virgin olive oil

Chop basil, parsley, Parmesan, lemon juice, salt and garlic finely in a food processor. Drizzle in olive oil with motor running. Place in a clean, dry container; cover tightly and keep refrigerated or frozen until needed.

Makes 1^1/$_2$ cups (375 mL).

Tip: Divide pesto mixture between the spaces in an ice cube tray. Freeze solid. Transfer cubes to a zip-top bag. Each cube is the equivalent of about 2 tbsp (30 mL) pesto.

Green Goddess Dressing and Dip

fast fix

healthier choice

make-ahead

This healthy dressing is great on tomato and lettuce salads or as the centerpiece for a crudité platter.

1	ripe avocado, about 8 oz (500 g)
3/4 cup (175 mL)	water
1 tsp (5 mL)	finely grated lime peel
3 tbsp (45 mL)	lime juice
1/2 tsp (2 mL)	ground cumin
1/2 tsp (2 mL)	salt
1/4 tsp (1 mL)	pepper
2	green onions, chopped
1	clove garlic

Halve avocado. Peel, and remove stone. Chop flesh and place in a blender. Add water, lime peel, lime juice, cumin, salt, pepper, green onions and garlic. Blend until smooth. Taste and adjust seasoning if necessary. Keeps, covered and refrigerated, for up to 3 days.

Makes 1 1/4 cups (300 mL).

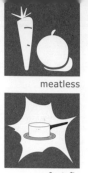

meatless

fast fix

Shirley Valentine Salad on Crunchy Herb Toast

This salad combines a lighter version of a traditional Greek salad with a bruschetta base for a satisfying appetizer or side dish.

1/3	baguette, sliced into long, thin pieces
1 tbsp (15 mL)	chopped fresh oregano or 1/2 tsp (2 mL) dried oregano
1 tbsp (15 mL)	white wine vinegar
1 tsp (5 mL)	grated lemon peel
1	clove garlic, minced
1/4 tsp (1 mL)	each salt and pepper
pinch	granulated sugar
1/4 cup (50 mL)	extra virgin olive oil
3	plum tomatoes
2 cups (500 mL)	finely chopped English cucumber
1/2 cup (125 mL)	finely diced red onion
1/2 cup (125 mL)	pitted, chopped Gaeta or kalamata olives
	crumbled feta cheese (optional)

Spread sliced bread on a baking tray and lightly toast on both sides under the broiler. Set aside. Combine oregano with vinegar, lemon peel, garlic, salt, pepper and sugar in a large bowl. Whisking, stir in olive oil.

Halve tomatoes lengthwise and squeeze out seeds. Chop finely and add to dressing mixture. Add cucumber, onion and olives and toss to combine.

Lay a slice of toast on each serving plate or down the length of a serving platter. Spoon vegetable mixture over center of toasts. Crumble feta cheese over top (if using).

Makes 6 servings.

Jicama and Orange Salad

fast but fancy

pantry plus

Jicama may look weird but it adds an exciting crunch to this salad.

1/2 cup (125 mL)	orange juice
1 tsp (5 mL)	finely chopped crystallized ginger
1 tbsp (15 mL)	rice wine vinegar
1/4 tsp (1 mL)	salt
1/4 tsp (1 mL)	cayenne pepper
1 tbsp (15 mL)	toasted sesame oil
2 tbsp (30 mL)	vegetable oil
1	jicama, about 1 1/2 lbs (750 g)
1 cup (250 mL)	peeled, thinly sliced red onion
2	oranges
4 cups (1 L)	baby spinach (1 bag)
2 tbsp (30 mL)	toasted sesame seeds

Combine orange juice with ginger, rice wine vinegar, salt and cayenne. Whisk in sesame and vegetable oils. Reserve.

Peel jicama and slice into 2-inch (5-cm) long thin strips. Combine with onions and just enough dressing to coat. Cover and reserve in refrigerator.

Hold whole oranges on cutting board and slice away peels and white pith using a sharp knife. Cut between membranes to make segments. Combine with spinach and jicama in a bowl; drizzle dressing over mixture. Toss gently until evenly coated. Sprinkle with toasted sesame seeds.

Makes 6 to 8 servings.

pantry plus

light

fast but fancy

Watermelon, Radish and Cucumber Salad

A novel summer salad that tastes as great as it looks.

1 tbsp (15 mL)	white wine vinegar
¼ tsp (1 mL)	Dijon mustard
¼ tsp (1 mL)	each salt and pepper
¼ cup (50 mL)	extra virgin olive oil
2 cups (500 mL)	diced seedless watermelon
1	English cucumber, quartered and chopped into bite-size pieces
1 cup (250 mL)	diced radishes
	Boston lettuce leaves

Whisk white wine vinegar with mustard, salt and pepper in a small bowl. Whisking, drizzle in oil until well combined (taste and add up to ¼ tsp/1 mL granulated sugar if too tangy). Reserve dressing.

Prepare watermelon, cucumber and radishes and combine in a large bowl. Can be prepared to this point, covered, and reserved in the refrigerator for up to 6 hours.

Drizzle dressing over salad and toss to combine just before serving. Place a Boston lettuce leaf on individual salad plates or line a deep platter with enough leaves to cover. Spoon salad mixture into leaves.

Makes 4 to 6 servings.

Asian Pear and Pecan Salad

fast but fancy

pantry plus

This salad is a swish sort of dish that's sure to make an impression at the dinner table.

1 cup (250 mL)	cranberry juice
2 tbsp (30 mL)	tamari or soy sauce
2	cloves garlic, minced
1 tsp (5 mL)	Dijon mustard
1/2 tsp (2 mL)	each salt and pepper
2 tbsp (30 mL)	extra virgin olive oil
2	large Asian pears, cored and sliced
3	green onions, chopped
1/3 cup (75 mL)	finely chopped celery
1/3 cup (75 mL)	dried cranberries
2 cups (500 mL)	baby spinach leaves
1/4 cup (50 mL)	toasted pecan pieces

Combine cranberry juice and tamari or soy sauce in a small saucepan. Bring to a boil and simmer rapidly for about 10 minutes or until reduced and syrupy.

Remove from heat and stir in garlic, mustard, salt and pepper. Drizzle in oil while whisking constantly.

Mix pears with green onions, celery and cranberries. Add dressing and spinach. Toss to combine. Sprinkle with pecans.

Makes 6 servings.

fast fix

fast but fancy

Fall Greens with Roasted Tomatoes

Inspired by autumn colors, this salad is a truly lovely way to start a meal.

3 cups (750 mL)	lightly packed endive
3 cups (750 mL)	lightly packed arugula leaves
1 cup (250 mL)	lightly packed shredded radicchio
2 tbsp (30 mL)	red wine vinegar
1 tbsp (15 mL)	finely chopped fresh thyme
1/2 tsp (2 mL)	Dijon mustard
1 tsp (5 mL)	honey or granulated sugar
1/2 tsp (2 mL)	each salt and pepper
1/2 cup (125 mL)	extra virgin olive oil
2 cups (500 mL)	red or yellow cherry tomatoes, hulls removed, halved

Wash lettuces and tear into bite-size pieces. Place in a large bowl.

Whisk vinegar with thyme, mustard, honey or sugar, salt and pepper. Whisking constantly, drizzle in olive oil. Place tomatoes in a bowl and toss with half the dressing.

Heat a skillet over medium-high heat. Turn tomato mixture into hot pan and cook, stirring, for 2 to 3 minutes or until skins start to break.

Add tomatoes to greens and toss with remaining dressing.

Makes 8 servings.

Hearts of Romaine Salad with Whole Grain Mustard Vinaigrette

pantry plus

make-ahead

This pretty salad, adorned with a tangy dressing, is a perfect partner for creamy pasta dishes.

1 tbsp (15 mL)	white wine vinegar
½ tsp (2 mL)	whole grain Dijon mustard
½ tsp (2 mL)	dried thyme
½ tsp (2 mL)	each salt and pepper
½ tsp (2 mL)	granulated sugar
1	small clove garlic, minced
¼ cup (50 mL)	extra virgin olive oil
2	romaine hearts
1 cup (250 mL)	quartered cherry tomatoes

Whisk vinegar with mustard, thyme, salt, pepper, sugar and garlic in a bowl. Whisking, drizzle in oil and mix until well combined. Add tomatoes and toss to coat.

Cut each romaine heart lengthwise into quarters. Arrange on a round platter with points facing out. Using a slotted spoon, remove tomatoes from vinaigrette and arrange in the center of the lettuce. Drizzle dressing over romaine spears.

Makes 8 servings.

Tip: Make dressing up to 2 days ahead; cover and refrigerate. Bring to room temperature before serving.

healthier choice

fast but fancy

meatless

Shrimp-Filled Salad Rolls

More refreshing than a traditional spring roll, these salad rolls are easy to make and taste terrific, too.

1 tbsp (15 mL)	rice vinegar
1 tbsp (15 mL)	lime juice
1 tsp (5 mL)	liquid honey
1/2 tsp (2 mL)	finely grated lime peel
1/4 tsp (1 mL)	crushed hot pepper flakes
1 tbsp (15 mL)	sesame oil
1 tbsp (15 mL)	vegetable oil
2 tbsp (30 mL)	chopped fresh coriander or parsley
1/2 tsp (2 mL)	each salt and pepper
1 lb (500 g)	peeled, cooked small shrimp, tails removed
1/4 cup (50 mL)	finely diced red onion
1 cup (250 mL)	bean sprouts
6	Boston lettuce leaves

Tip: If using frozen cooked shrimp, thaw quickly by placing in a colander and running under cold water for 5 minutes. Drain well before using.

Whisk rice vinegar with lime juice, honey, lime peel and crushed red pepper flakes in a large bowl. Whisking constantly, drizzle in sesame and vegetable oils until well combined. Stir in coriander or parsley, salt and pepper.

Add shrimp and onion to bowl. Toss until well combined. Reserve. Stir bean sprouts into shrimp mixture. Taste and adjust seasoning if necessary. Cut tough stem ends from lettuce leaves and lay flat. Spoon equal amounts of shrimp mixture onto the end of each lettuce leaf; roll up to encase mixture and secure with a toothpick.

Makes 6 servings.

Green Goddess Dressing and Dip, page 65

Fall Greens with Roasted Tomatoes, page 70

Vineyard Chicken Salad, page 77

Cheese and Cracker Chicken, page 95

Warm Red Snapper Salad

This quick and easy dish is perfect for a snazzy lunch or as a starter for a summer dinner party.

6 cups (1.5 L)	mesclun greens
2 tbsp (30 mL)	sherry or white wine vinegar
1/2 tsp (2 mL)	Dijon mustard
1/2 tsp (2 mL)	crushed pink peppercorns
1/4 tsp (2 mL)	granulated sugar
3/4 tsp (4 mL)	each salt and pepper
1/3 cup (75 mL)	extra virgin olive oil
1 tbsp (15 mL)	butter
1 tbsp (15 mL)	vegetable oil
1	clove garlic, thinly sliced
12 oz (350 g)	red snapper fillet

Place greens in a shallow bowl. Whisk vinegar with mustard, peppercorns, sugar and 1/4 tsp (1 mL) each salt and pepper in small bowl or measuring cup. Drizzle in olive oil, whisking constantly. Reserve.

Heat butter with vegetable oil in a large skillet set over medium heat; add garlic and cook, stirring often, for 3 minutes or until fragrant and turning brown. Remove garlic from pan and discard.

Increase heat to medium-high; sprinkle remaining 1/2 tsp (2 mL) of salt and pepper evenly over fish. Cook, turning once using a large metal spatula, for 5 minutes or until golden on fleshy side. Place, skin side up, under broiler for 2 minutes or until crisp.

Transfer fish to a cutting board and slice into long strips. Arrange over greens. Place skillet back on burner and pour in reserved dressing; stir to scrape up any cooked-on bits. Drizzle over salad and serve immediately.

Makes 4 servings.

pantry trick

fast but fancy

meatless

Smoked Tuna Couscous Salad

This no-oven-supper is satisfying and chic all at once.

1 cup (250 mL)	instant couscous
1¼ cups (300 mL)	boiling chicken or vegetable broth
½ cup (125 mL)	chopped pimento or roasted red peppers
¼ cup (50 mL)	lightly packed fresh parsley leaves
2 tbsp (30 mL)	lemon juice
2 tbsp (30 mL)	pomegranate molasses
½ tsp (2 mL)	each salt and pepper
½ tsp (2 mL)	granulated sugar
¼ tsp (1 mL)	paprika
⅓ cup (75 mL)	extra virgin olive oil
1	tomato, seeded and chopped
2	green onions, thinly sliced
1 cup (250 mL)	finely chopped cucumber
2 cans (120 g)	smoked tuna fillets or flake light tuna, in chunks

Place couscous in a large bowl. Pour in broth. Cover and let stand for 5 minutes. Fluff with a fork and cool slightly.

For dressing, place pimento or peppers in a blender or food processor. Add parsley, lemon juice, pomegranate molasses, salt, pepper, sugar, paprika and oil. Blend until smooth.

Stir dressing, tomatoes, green onions, cucumbers and tuna. Toss with couscous until evenly mixed. Taste and adjust seasoning if necessary.

Makes 4 servings.

Green Curry Tuna Salad

Wake up your taste buds with this bold new take on tuna salad.

1/4 cup (50 mL)	mayonnaise
1/4 cup (50 ml)	sour cream, yogurt or mayonnaise
2 tsp (10 mL)	Thai green curry paste
1	celery stalk, chopped
1	green apple, cored and chopped
2 tbsp (30 mL)	chopped fresh parsley (optional)
1 can (6.5 oz/184 g)	water packed tuna
	salt

Stir mayonnaise with sour cream, yogurt or more mayonnaise, curry paste, celery, apple and parsley (if using) until evenly combined. Drain tuna and flake using a fork. Add to mayonnaise mixture and stir until evenly combined.

Taste and season with salt. Serve as a sandwich filling or as part of a salad plate.

Makes about 2 cups (500 mL).

pantry trick

fast fix

meatless

meatless

healthier choice

fast fix

Poached Egg Salad

Serving poached eggs on greens creates a new, lighter solution to suppertime dilemmas.

Dressing:

1 tbsp (15 mL)	white wine vinegar
1/2 tsp (2 mL)	chopped fresh thyme or pinch dried thyme
pinch	granulated sugar or 1/4 tsp (1 mL) liquid honey
1/4 tsp	each salt and pepper
1/4 cup (50 mL)	extra virgin olive oil

Salad:

4 cups (1.5 L)	mixed salad greens
1	tomato, sliced
1 tsp (5 mL)	salt
1 tsp (5 mL)	vinegar
4	eggs

Dressing:

Combine vinegar, thyme, sugar, salt and pepper in a large bowl. Whisk in olive oil.

Salad:

Drizzle greens with dressing and toss to combine untill evenly coated. Divide greens evenly between plates and top with a slice of tomato. Reserve. Bring a large saucepan of water to a boil. Stir in salt and vinegar. Break each egg into a small bowl or large spoon and gently add to boiling water. Stir the water immediately with the handle of a spoon or a chopstick. Cook eggs for 2 to 5 minutes or until as firm as desired.

Lift eggs out of water using a slotted spoon. Drain by placing spoon on a paper towel for a few moments. Place a poached egg on or next to each tomato slice.

Makes 2 to 4 servings.

Vineyard Chicken Salad

This salad makes a great centerpiece for a patio supper.

6 oz. (175 g)	cooked, skinless, boneless chicken breast
4 tsp (20 mL)	light or regular mayonnaise
2 tbsp (30 mL)	chopped fresh basil or coriander
1/2 cup (125 mL)	halved seedless red or green grapes
	salt and pepper

Cut chicken into small cubes and place in a bowl. Add mayonnaise and basil or coriander. Stir until well combined. Taste and add salt and pepper as needed. Gently stir in grapes. (Can be made to this point, covered and refrigerated for up to 1 day.) Just before serving taste and adjust seasoning. Serve divided between two pitas or mounded into cantaloupe halves.

Makes 2 servings as a main course or enough filling for 4 sandwiches.

pantry trick

leftover wizard

Curried Mango Chicken Salad

Great on its own, in a sandwich or as part of a salad plate.

1/3 cup (75 mL)	light or regular mayonnaise
2 tsp (10 mL)	mild Indian curry paste
1 tsp (5 mL)	white wine vinegar
1 tsp (5 mL)	minced ginger root
1/2 tsp (2 mL)	grated lime peel
1 tsp (5 mL)	lime juice
3 cups (750 mL)	diced, cooked chicken
1 cup (250 mL)	peeled, diced mango
2	green onions, chopped
	salt and pepper
2 tbsp (30 mL)	toasted slivered almonds (optional)

Stir mayonnaise with curry paste, vinegar, ginger, lime peel and lime juice in a large bowl. Stir in chicken, mango and onions. Taste and add salt and pepper as necessary. Just before serving, sprinkle over almonds (if using).

Makes 4 servings.

Variation:

Substitute 1/4 cup (50 mL) rehydrated raisins for mango.

leftover wizard

fast fix

Exceptionally Easy Curried Chicken Salad

This quick fix recipe turns filling a lunch box into a positive experience.

¼ cup (50 mL)	light or regular mayonnaise
1 tsp (5 mL)	mild Indian curry paste
1 tsp (5 mL)	mango chutney
2 cups (500 mL)	diced cooked chicken
	salt and pepper

Stir mayonnaise with curry paste and chutney. Toss with chicken until evenly coated. Add salt and pepper to taste.

Makes enough filling for 4 sandwiches.

pantry plus

fast but fancy

Chicken Salad Chinois

Asian flavors perk up this easy concoction that combines leftover chicken with pantry staples to create an exotic taste.

1/3 cup (75 mL)	orange juice
1/4 cup (50 mL)	peanut butter
1 tbsp (15 mL)	soy sauce
1 tbsp (15 mL)	hoisin sauce
1/2 tsp (2 mL)	minced ginger root
1	small clove garlic, minced
1/4 cup (50 mL)	lightly packed coriander leaves
3 cups (750 mL)	diced cooked chicken
1 cup (250 mL)	diced cucumber
1	tomato, chopped
1/2 cup (125 mL)	bean sprouts (optional)

Tip: Great served in a pita with lettuce or on a bed of baby spinach leaves.

Stir orange juice, peanut butter, soy sauce, hoisin, ginger and garlic until smooth. Stir in coriander leaves.

Mix chicken, cucumber, tomato and bean sprouts (if using) in a large bowl. Stir in orange juice dressing until everything is evenly coated.

Makes 4 servings.

Warm Soba Noodle and Broccoli Salad

meatless

pantry plus

Soba noodles are a delicious Japanese buckwheat invention. Whole-wheat pasta makes an acceptable substitute but it's heavier and lacks the refinement soba lends to this dish.

1 pkg (300 g)	dry soba noodles or whole wheat spaghetti
4 cups (1 L)	broccoli florets
1/4 cup (50 mL)	tamari or light soy sauce
2 tbsp (30 mL)	minced ginger root
1 tbsp (15 mL)	lime juice
1/2 tsp (2 mL)	hot sauce
1/2 tsp (2 mL)	brown sugar
2 tbsp (30 mL)	toasted sesame oil
1/4 cup (50 mL)	vegetable oil
3	plum tomatoes or 1 beefsteak tomato, seeded and chopped
2 tbsp (30 mL)	toasted slivered almonds (optional)
	salt and pepper
	lime wedges

Cook pasta for 5 minutes in a large pot of boiling salted water. Add broccoli and cook until noodles are al dente, about 2 minutes. (If using whole wheat noodles cook for 10 to 12 minutes, adding broccoli in the last 2 minutes.) Drain well.

Whisk tamari or soy sauce with ginger, lime juice, hot sauce and brown sugar in a large serving bowl. Whisking constantly, drizzle in sesame and vegetable oils. Add tomato, broccoli and noodles and toss gently to combine. Sprinkle nuts (if using) over top of salad. Taste and add salt and pepper according to preference. Serve with a lime wedge on the side.

Makes 4 servings.

Variations:

Add 1 to 2 cups (250 to 500 mL) shredded cooked chicken or lightly sautéed firm tofu for additional protein.

Main Courses

Roman Fritatta

meatless

pantry trick

Not quite a Roman holiday, but a nice change from meat and potatoes, nonetheless!

1 tsp (5 mL)	vegetable oil
1	small onion, peeled, halved and sliced
1pkg (300 g)	thawed, well-drained frozen chopped spinach or 1 cup (250 mL) cooked, chopped spinach
1/4 cup (50 mL)	golden raisins
1/4 tsp (1 mL)	cayenne pepper
10	eggs, beaten
1/4 cup (50 mL)	milk
1/2 tsp (2 mL)	Dijon mustard
1/2 tsp (2 mL)	each salt and pepper
1 cup (250 mL)	shredded mozzarella cheese or four-cheese blend
1 tbsp (15 mL)	toasted pine nuts

Tip: This recipe (and the following egg recipes) work well and are even faster to put together if you use pasteurized liquid eggs. Substitute 1 carton (250 mL) liquid pasteurized eggs for every 5 eggs in the shell.

Preheat oven to 375°F (190°C). Lightly grease a 9-inch (23-cm) glass pie plate or casserole. Heat oil in a non-stick skillet set over medium heat. Add the onion; cook, stirring often, for 5 minutes. Add the spinach, raisins and cayenne pepper. Reserve.

Whisk eggs with milk, mustard, salt and pepper. Stir in onion mixture and cheese then pour into prepared pie plate. Sprinkle pine nuts over top.

Bake in center of preheated oven for 25 to 30 minutes or until set in the center and golden brown. Let stand for 5 minutes before slicing.

Makes 8 servings.

family favorite

meatless

Mushroom Egg Foo Yung

This dish is great for a quick weeknight supper or as part of a full Chinese-style family dinner.

1 cup (250 mL)	vegetable or chicken broth
1 tsp (5 mL)	light soy sauce
1 tsp (5 mL)	oyster sauce
1 tbsp (15 mL)	cornstarch
10	eggs or 2 cartons (250 mL each) liquid eggs
1/2 tsp (2 mL)	each salt and pepper
3 tbsp (45 mL)	vegetable oil
1	onion, peeled and thinly sliced
2 cups (500 mL)	sliced mushrooms
1/2 cup (125 mL)	bean sprouts
1	small clove garlic, minced
1 tsp (5 mL)	minced ginger root
2	green onions, sliced

Stir vegetable or chicken broth with soy sauce, oyster sauce and cornstarch. Reserve. Beat eggs lightly with salt and pepper. Reserve.

Heat 1 tbsp (15 mL) oil in a non-stick wok or skillet set over medium heat; add onion and cook, stirring often, for 5 minutes or until softened. Increase heat to high; add remaining oil and mushrooms and stir-fry for 3 to 5 minutes or until lightly browned.

Stir in bean sprouts, garlic and ginger. Push mushroom mixture up sides of wok or to edge of pan. Pour egg mixture into center of wok; cook, stirring often, for 60 seconds or until mixture is becoming chunky. Cover and cook for 2 minutes or until egg is set and bottom is golden brown. Turn out onto a deep platter or shallow pasta bowl and tent with foil.

Stir cornstarch mixture well and pour into wok. Cook, stirring, for 1 to 2 minutes or until lightly thickened. Pour over egg mixture. Sprinkle green onions over dish.

Makes 4 to 6 servings.

Variations:

Chicken: Omit mushrooms and add 1½ cups (375 mL) diced, cooked chicken.

Rainbow: Omit mushrooms. Substitute ½ cup (125 mL) each sliced red, green and orange peppers

pantry trick

family favorite

make-ahead

Strata-Various 1-2-3

Using leftovers from the refrigerator, three-step stratas can be thrown together for dinner in minutes and then cooked while you set the table and sort through the mail. Feel free to mix and match ingredients according to what you have on hand. A handful of suggestions follows.

3 cups (750 mL)	cubed bread
1 cup (250 mL)	finely diced ham
1 cup (250 mL)	shredded Swiss cheese
2	green onions, thinly sliced on diagonal
2 cups (500 mL)	cooked broccoli florets
5	eggs, beaten
1½ cups (375 mL)	milk
½ tsp (2 mL)	each salt and pepper

Preheat oven to 350°F (180°C). Lightly oil a 10-inch (25-cm) pie plate or shallow casserole dish. Spread bread cubes evenly in dish.

Sprinkle over ham, cheese, green onions and broccoli. In a bowl, whisk eggs with milk, salt and pepper. Pour evenly over bread mixture.

Bake in center of preheated oven for 30 to 40 minutes or until set and golden. Let rest for 10 minutes before slicing and serving.

Makes 6 to 8 servings.

Variations:

California: Substitute leftover chicken for ham, use Monterey Jack cheese for Swiss and add 2 seeded, chopped tomatoes for broccoli.

Stampede: Substitute chopped cooked steak for ham and cheddar for Swiss cheese. Add 1 tsp (5 mL) chili powder to milk mixture.

Florentine: Skip the meat. Squeeze the water from 1 pkg (340 g) thawed frozen chopped spinach. Substitute mozzarella for Swiss cheese and 2 seeded, chopped tomatoes for broccoli.

Uptown: Substitute smoked salmon for ham and asparagus tips for broccoli. Add 1 tbsp (15 mL) chopped fresh dill or 1/2 tsp (2 mL) dried dillweed to the egg mixture.

fast but fancy

meatless

Bombay Spiced Egg Casserole

Revive your interest in eggs for supper with this new twist.

10	eggs, beaten
1/4 cup (50 mL)	milk
1 tsp (5 mL)	minced fresh ginger root
1/2 tsp (2 mL)	ground cumin
1/4 tsp (1 mL)	each salt and pepper
2	large or 4 plum tomatoes, seeded and finely diced

Topping:

1 cup (250 mL)	fresh bread crumbs, from about 2 bread slices
1/4 cup (50 mL)	grated Parmesan cheese
2 tbsp (30 mL)	finely chopped fresh coriander or parsley
1 tsp (5 mL)	finely grated fresh lime or lemon peel
1/4 tsp (1 mL)	each salt and pepper
2 tbsp (30 mL)	butter, melted

Preheat oven to 325°F (160°C). Lightly butter an 11 x 7-inch (1.5-L) baking dish or 9-inch (23-cm) square baking pan. In a bowl whisk eggs with milk, ginger, cumin, salt and pepper. Stir in tomatoes. Pour into baking dish.

Combine bread crumbs, cheese, coriander or parsley, citrus peel, salt and pepper. Sprinkle evenly over egg mixture. Drizzle evenly with melted butter. Bake in center of preheated oven for 35 minutes or until eggs are set. Broil for 1 to 2 minutes if topping isn't golden. Cool for 5 minutes before slicing and serving.

Makes 4 to 6 servings.

Egg-Topped Portobello Bakes

pantry plus

fast but fancy

meatless

The meaty texture of portobello mushrooms makes this a great dinner for occasional and transitional vegetarians. Serve with crusty bread and a salad for a complete dinner.

4	giant portobello mushrooms, each about 4 inches (10 cm) in diameter
1 tbsp (15 mL)	olive oil
2 tbsp (30 mL)	balsamic vinegar
1/4 tsp (2 mL)	each salt and pepper
4 tsp (20 mL)	basil pesto
4	eggs

Preheat oven to 375°F (190°C). Remove the stem ends from mushrooms and wipe off any clinging dirt. Using a spoon, deepen the cavity where the stem attaches to the mushroom so that it leaves a depression large enough to hold a whole egg in its shell.

Whisk oil with balsamic vinegar, salt and pepper. Brush evenly all over portobello mushrooms. Place mushrooms, gill side down, on a lightly oiled baking tray; bake in a pre-heated 375°F (190°C) oven for 5 minutes.

Turn over mushrooms and, using the back of a spoon, spread pesto over mushrooms. Break an egg into each mushroom cap and return pan to oven. Bake for 8 to 10 minutes or until egg is desired doneness. Taste and season to taste with additional salt and pepper if necessary.

Makes 2 to 4 servings.

Tip: If you dislike the dark juices cooked portobello mushrooms release, scoop out and discard gills of mushrooms before cooking.

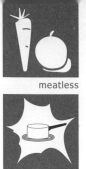

meatless

fast fix

Egg Fajitas

Imagine a Western sandwich morphed into a traditional fajita and you get this quick supper.

1 tbsp (15 mL)	vegetable oil
1	onion, peeled and thinly sliced
2	red or green peppers, sliced
2 tsp (10 mL)	chili powder
1/2 tsp (2 mL)	each salt and pepper
6	eggs, beaten
2 tbsp (30 mL)	finely chopped fresh coriander or parsley (optional)
4	large wheat flour tortillas
1/4 cup (50 mL)	shredded Monterey Jack or sharp cheddar cheese
	salsa (optional)
	sour cream (optional)

Heat oil in a non-stick skillet set over medium heat. Add onion and cook, stirring often, for 5 minutes. Increase heat to medium-high. Add peppers, 1 tsp (5 mL) chili powder, salt and pepper. Cook, stirring often, for 5 to 10 minutes or until well browned.

Add eggs and cook, stirring gently and folding over, until eggs are softly set, about 5 minutes. Sprinkle over remaining chili powder and coriander or parsley (if using).

Spread tortillas on dinner plates. Divide egg mixture evenly among tortillas. Sprinkle cheese evenly over each fajita, fold one side up to make a flap and then start rolling from an adjoining side to encase mixture. Serve with salsa and sour cream on the side if desired.

Makes 4 servings.

Lifeline Frozen Pizza

family favorite

pantry plus

leftover wizard

Turn leftovers into pizza classics. Using this easy food processor dough recipe, store-bought dough or a prepared pizza base, turn leftovers into make-ahead frozen dinner solutions.

1 1/2 cups (375 mL)	all-purpose flour
1 tsp (5 mL)	quick rising yeast
3/4 tsp (4 mL)	salt
1 tbsp (15 mL)	honey
1 1/2 tsp (7 mL)	olive oil or butter
1/2 cup (125 mL)	very warm water

Blend flour, yeast and salt in food processor fitted with a metal blade; add honey and oil or butter. With motor running, drizzle in water; mix for 2 minutes or until ball forms. Remove from processor.

Knead dough into a smooth ball; place in lightly oiled bowl, turning to coat all over. Cover and let rise for 30 minutes. Roll dough into a circle about 12 inches (33 cm) in diameter and transfer to a lightly floured pizza pan or baking sheet; fold under edge to make a rim. Cover with toppings (see below). Wrap well with plastic wrap and freeze for up to 3 weeks. (Bake from frozen.)

To serve:

Preheat oven to 450°F (225°C). Slide pizza off pan and onto lower oven rack. Bake for 25 minutes or until golden and crisp on the bottom. Slide onto a cutting board. Let rest for 2 to 3 minutes before slicing.

Makes 8 slices.

Basic topping proportions:

1/2 cup (125 mL)	pizza or spaghetti sauce
2 1/2 cups (625 mL)	mixed toppings such as: cooked or freshly sliced vegetables, cooked shredded chicken, chopped ham, etc.
1 1/2 cups (375 mL)	shredded mozzarella or other cheese blend, about 6 oz (180 g)

Continued on next page...

Perfect Pizza Combos

	Toppings	Cheese	Special notes
Classic	Pepperoni and mushrooms	mozzarella	
Zesty	Sautéed or grilled peppers and 1 cooked, thinly sliced hot Italian sausage or 1 jar (6 oz/170 mL) marinated artichokes, drained	1 roll (113 g) soft goat cheese	Stir 1 tbsp (15 mL) pesto into sauce
Over the Swiss Border	1 cup (250 mL) Sublimely Delicious Caramelized Onions (see page 165)	Gruyère	Omit tomato sauce and lightly brush crust with olive oil
Asian	Stir-fry leftovers	1/2 cup (125 mL) grated Parmesan cheese	Omit tomato sauce
Sunny side up	Sprinkle with 1/4 cup (50 mL) diced ham. Break 6 eggs over top. Sprinkle with salt and pepper and gently transfer pizza on pan to oven.	1 cup (250 mL) mozzarella	Substitute 1/4 cup (50 mL) sun-dried tomato paste for sauce. Sprinkle cheese over sauce and then add toppings.
Texas	Meat or bean chili, green pepper slices	cheddar	Omit tomato sauce
Pear Dessert	1 (14 oz/398 mL) can sliced pears, drained	1/4 cup (50 mL) chopped walnuts or pecans	Omit tomato sauce and brush crust with melted butter and 1/4 cup (50 mL) brown sugar mixed with 1/2 tsp (2 mL) each ground ginger and cinnamon

Weeknight Roasted Flat Chicken

family favorite

pantry plus

Although roasted chicken can be delicious prepared with only salt and pepper, the variations below are almost as simple to prepare but taste like you fussed for hours.

| 3 to 4 lb (1.5 to 2 kg) | flattened roasting chicken |
| 1/2 tsp (2 mL) | each salt and pepper |

Preheat oven to 450°F (225°C). Rinse flattened chicken with cold running water and pat dry with paper towel. Place on a rimmed baking sheet just large enough to hold bird. Sprinkle evenly with salt and pepper.

Roast on center rack in preheated oven, basting occasionally with pan juices, until an instant read thermometer inserted in thickest part of the breast registers 180°F (85°C) and the legs feel wobbly, from 40 to 45 minutes.

Turn off the oven. Brush bird evenly with pan juices and let rest in the oven for 10 minutes before carving.

Makes 4 servings with leftovers for lunch.

Tip: To flatten a roasting chicken: Hold a whole chicken with the neck cavity balanced on a cutting board and the back facing you. Use a sharp heavy knife to cut down one side of the backbone. Rotate the chicken 90 degrees and cut along the other side of the backbone until it comes free. Spread out the chicken, breast side up. Using a boning knife, slide the tip under the rib cage and, using small strokes, cut the breast away from the meat. Turn the chicken over and use the knife to make small slits in the loose skin around what used to be the large cavity. Push the legs up under the wings and insert the knuckle of the drumstick through slits to hold legs in place. Discard or reserve back bone and rib cage for making chicken broth. Or, if removing the breastbone is too much fuss, spread the backbone-less chicken out, breast side up, and use a mallet to gently flatten the breastbone so that the chicken lies flat. If you don't have a mallet, rest the bottom of a heavy skillet on the breastbone and press down with the weight of your hands to break it.

Variations:

Pesto

½ tsp (2 mL)	each salt and pepper
½ cup (125 mL)	basil pesto

Brush pesto mixture evenly all over chicken before roasting.

Pomegranate Glazed

3 tbsp (45 mL)	pomegranate molasses
1 tbsp (15 mL)	orange juice concentrate or juice
1 tbsp (15 mL)	balsamic vinegar
1 tbsp (15 mL)	finely chopped fresh mint or rosemary
1 tsp (5 mL)	black pepper
1 tsp (5 mL)	brown sugar
½ tsp (2 mL)	each ground cumin and coriander
3	cloves garlic, minced
¾ tsp (4 mL)	salt

Combine all ingredients. Brush evenly all over chicken after first 20 minutes of roasting. Baste frequently.

Buttermilk Basted

¾ cup (175 mL)	buttermilk or yogurt
2 tbsp (30 mL)	Dijon mustard
1 tbsp (15 mL)	freshly grated lemon peel
1 tbsp (15 mL)	vegetable oil
1	clove garlic, minced
1 tsp (5 mL)	ground black pepper

Combine ingredients and marinate chicken for at least 30 minutes. Chicken can be placed in marinade in a zip-top bag and frozen for up to 3 weeks. Defrost overnight in refrigerator before roasting.

Roast as directed in main method, basting often.

Mahogany Marinated

1/2 cup (125 mL)	light soy sauce
2 tbsp (30 mL)	toasted sesame oil
1/4 cup (50 mL)	brown sugar
2	cloves garlic, minced

Combine all ingredients. Marinate chicken for 30 minutes or for up to 2 days. (Chicken can be placed in marinade in a zip-top bag and frozen for up to 3 weeks. Defrost overnight in refrigerator before roasting.)

Roast as directed in main method, basting often with pan juices.

Cheese and Cracker Chicken

1 cup (250 mL)	coarse salted cracker crumbs
1/2 cup (125 mL)	shredded hard cheese such as aged cheddar, Parmesan or Asiago
1/2 tsp (2 mL)	pepper
1	egg, beaten

Combine crackers and cheese in a heavy plastic bag until well mixed. Brush egg all over chicken. Lay chicken on roasting pan and sprinkle evenly with pepper. Press crumb mixture all over chicken.

Roast as directed in main method. Tent chicken with foil part-way through cooking if crumbs become too dark.

Tip: Crumbs can be made using a rolling pin or food processor. The crumbs and the cheese should be fine enough to coat the chicken evenly but not as fine as dry bread crumbs.

Mother Hubbard's Gourmet Flat Chicken

Brush 1/2 cup (125 mL) of your favorite bottled or home-made vinaigrette over chicken before roasting.

Tip: These mixtures can also be used when preparing chicken strips, bone-in or boneless pieces of chicken:

For boneless breasts, preheat oven to 400°F (200°C) and bake for 20 to 25 minutes or until no longer pink in center.

For chicken strips, preheat oven to 400°F (200°C) and bake for 15 minutes or until no longer pink in the center.

For bone-in pieces such as legs, preheat oven to 400°F (200°C) and bake for 30 to 35 minutes or until juices run clear when flesh is pierced.

fast fix

leftover wizard

Basil-Balsamic Chicken and Pasta Toss

Although this recipe originated as a way to use up leftover pasta, it's also very good served over couscous.

1	large chicken breast, about 8 oz (500 g)
1/4 tsp (2 mL)	salt
1/4 tsp (2 mL)	pepper
1 tbsp (15 mL)	vegetable oil
3 tbsp (45 mL)	balsamic vinegar
1 cup (250 mL)	halved cherry or grape tomatoes
3 cups (750 mL)	cooked short pasta
1/4 cup (50 mL)	whole fresh basil leaves
1 tbsp (15 mL)	water
2 tbsp (30 mL)	shredded or grated Parmesan cheese

Tip: If serving with couscous or without pasta, add basil leaves with tomatoes and omit water.

Cut chicken into bite-size pieces. Sprinkle with salt and pepper. Heat oil in a non-stick skillet set over medium-high heat. Add chicken and cook for 2 minutes or until golden. Turn and cook for 2 minutes longer. Drizzle in balsamic vinegar and toss to coat. Add tomatoes and cook for 2 minutes longer. Stir in pasta and basil. Add water and cook, tossing, for 2 to 3 minutes or until heated through. Taste and adjust seasoning if necessary. Sprinkle with Parmesan cheese.

Makes 2 servings as a main course, or enough filling for 4 sandwiches.

The Ten Commandments of Steak Cooking

There truly is nothing simpler to make for dinner than a steak and a salad. Follow these easy directions to create a perfectly cooked steak every time.

1. Steaks to be cooked quickly in a skillet, on a grill, or under the broiler need to be tender cuts. Choose rib eye, filet mignon (tenderloin), strip loin, T-bone and porterhouse varieties.

2. For optimum tenderness, choose steaks that have plenty of marbled fat (don't worry, most of this fat renders out as the steak cooks, leaving only flavor and moisture behind, not extra calories) in the flesh and a modest amount of white fat (known as leaf fat) surrounding the flesh.

3. Avoid buying steaks that are cut thinner than 3/4-inch (1.5-cm) thick since they are often dry and difficult to sear without overcooking.

4. If steaks are very thick (more than 1 1/2 inches/4 cm) cut notches in the surrounding fat so that the steak doesn't curl as it cooks.

5. Bring steak to room temperature before cooking.

6. Preheat pan, grill, or broiling tray until almost smoking before adding meat.

7. Although marinating tender steaks is optional, all steaks taste better if lightly brushed with oil and sprinkled generously with salt and pepper just before cooking.

8. Place a 1-inch (2.5-cm) rib eye, porterhouse or T-bone steak on a hot pan or grill. Reduce heat to medium-high and cook, turning only once, for 6 to 7 minutes for rare, 9 to 12 minutes for medium and (I'm cringing, but if you must), 12 to 15 minutes for well-done (160°F/70°C).

9. Flank steaks benefit from being marinated overnight and should never be cooked beyond medium. Place a flank steak on a preheated pan and cook for 7 to 10 minutes, turning once. After resting, cut across the grain into thin strips.

10. Tenderloin or filet steaks should not be marinated for longer than 1 hour and, because they are so lean, should not be cooked beyond medium doneness. Place a 1-inch (2.5-cm) medallion of tenderloin on a preheated pan and cook, turning once, for about 5 minutes for rare or 6 to 7 minutes for medium.

family favorite

fast fix

make-ahead

In a Flash Meatballs

Whether you add these meatballs to tomato sauce or stack them on buns to make sandwiches, they strike a retro comfort food chord.

3 tbsp (45 mL)	basil pesto
1	small onion, peeled and finely grated
1	clove garlic, minced
½ tsp (2 mL)	salt
¼ tsp (1 mL)	pepper
1	egg, beaten
¼ cup (50 mL)	fresh bread crumbs
1 lb (500 g)	lean ground beef, chicken, lamb, veal or pork

Preheat oven to 350°F (180°C). Stir pesto with onion, garlic, salt, pepper and egg. Stir in bread crumbs. Crumble meat into bowl and toss gently with pesto mixture until evenly combined.

Turn meat mixture out on to a piece of plastic wrap or waxed paper. Use plastic to shape meat into a long even cylinder, about 1 inch (2.5 cm) in diameter. Unwrap and cut cylinder into 1-inch (2.5-cm) pieces. Use your hands to roll each section into a ball.

Place meatballs on a foil-lined rimmed baking sheet. Bake in preheated oven for 20 minutes or until internal temperature is 180°F (90°C).

Makes about 2 dozen meatballs.

Tips: If meat is difficult to roll into a cylinder, chill for 30 minutes.

Skillet method: Heat oil in a skillet set over medium-high heat. Add meatballs and brown, turning often, until evenly browned. Reduce heat to medium and cook, turning occasionally for 15 to 20 minutes or until internal temperature reaches 180°F (90°C).

Variations:

Ginger-scallion: Substitute 1/2 cup (125 mL) finely chopped green onions for grated onion. Omit pesto and add 1 tbsp (15 mL) minced ginger and 3 tbsp (45 mL) soy sauce to meat mixture. Ideal for ground beef or pork.

Texas: Omit pesto and add 2 tbsp (30 mL) grated Parmesan cheese, 1 tbsp (15 mL) chili powder and 2 tsp (10 mL) finely chopped fresh oregano or 1/2 tsp (2 mL) dried oregano (optional). Ideal with ground beef.

Moroccan: Omit pesto and add 1 tbsp (15 mL) finely chopped fresh mint, 1/2 tsp (4 mL) cinnamon, 1/2 tsp (2 mL) hot pepper sauce. Excellent with ground lamb, pork or chicken.

Lemon-dill: Omit pesto and add 1 tbsp (15 mL) chopped fresh dill or 1 tsp (5 mL) dried dill and 2 tsp (10 mL) finely grated lemon peel. Ideal with ground veal or chicken.

Mini meatloaves: Divide meat mixture evenly among 8 greased muffin tins, packing just tightly enough to make uniform-shaped loaves. Bake in a preheated 350°F (180°C) oven for 30 minutes or until no longer pink in the center.

pantry plus

fast but fancy

Châteaubriand for Two with Stilton-Port Sauce

Send the kids to grandma's, dim the lights and find the Barry White CD!

1 lb (500 g)	beef tenderloin roast or Châteaubriand
1 tbsp (15 mL)	melted butter
1/2 tsp (2 mL)	each salt and pepper
	Sauce:
1 tbsp (15 mL)	butter
1	large shallot or 1/4 onion, peeled and finely chopped
1	small clove garlic, minced
1/4 cup (50 mL)	port
1	sprig rosemary
1 tbsp (15 mL)	all-purpose flour
1 cup (250 mL)	beef or chicken broth
1/4 cup (50 mL)	Stilton or other blue cheese
	salt and pepper

Preheat oven to 500°F (260°C). Brush meat all over with melted butter and sprinkle evenly with salt and pepper.

Heat an ovenproof skillet over medium-high heat. Add meat and sear on all sides until browned. Transfer to preheated oven and roast for 20 minutes or until medium-rare (140°F/60°C on an instant read thermometer). Remove from oven and let rest on a platter for 5 minutes.

Sauce:

Place roasting skillet on stove over medium heat; melt butter and stir in shallots and garlic. Cook, stirring often, for 3 minutes or until softened. Stir in port and rosemary; bring to boil and cook for 2 minutes or until syrupy. Dust with flour, whisking to combine; cook for 1 minute. Stir in broth. Bring to boil and simmer for 5 minutes or until mixture coats the back of a spoon.

Strain sauce into a clean pan. Place over low heat. Stir crumbled cheese into sauce until smooth. Taste and adjust seasoning if necessary. Slice meat thickly and serve with sauce on the side.

Makes 2 servings.

pantry plus

make-ahead

South Pacific Flank Steak

I often marinate this delicious cut of meat on the weekend and then save it for a quick weeknight meal that cooks up in no time.

2 tbsp (30 mL)	fish sauce
2 tbsp (30 mL)	hoisin sauce
2 tbsp (30 mL)	lime juice
4 tsp (20 mL)	minced ginger root
1 tbsp (15 mL)	medium sherry
1 tsp (5 mL)	sesame oil
1/2 tsp (2 mL)	sambal oelek or chili-garlic sauce
2	cloves garlic, minced
1 lb (500 g)	flank steak

Tip: Prepare the marinade and steak as directed. Transfer to a zip-top bag and freeze for up to 1 month. Remove from the freezer and thaw in the refrigerator overnight. Proceed as directed above.

Whisk fish sauce with hoisin, lime juice, ginger, sherry, sesame oil, sambal oelek or chili-garlic sauce and garlic in a large, shallow bowl or zip-top bag. Add steak, turning to coat each side well with marinade. Cover and refrigerate for at least 6 hours or up to 4 days, turning meat occasionally. Bring to room temperature for 30 minutes.

Remove steak from marinade and place on a lightly greased hot grill or grill pan, preheated over medium-high heat. Cook, turning once, for 7 to 10 minutes or until medium rare. Transfer to a cutting board and let rest for 5 minutes. Slice very thinly across the grain using a carving or chef's knife.

Makes 4 servings.

Scallopini with Caper Sauce

This fast dish is quite light, making it a perfect opening act for a decadent dessert.

1 lb (500 g)	turkey or veal scallopini
2	eggs, beaten
2/3 cup (150 mL)	dry bread crumbs
1 tbsp (15 mL)	finely grated lemon peel
1 tsp (5 mL)	each salt and pepper
2 tbsp (30 mL)	olive oil (approx)
2 tsp (10 mL)	cold butter
2 tbsp (30 mL)	capers
2	cloves garlic, minced
1/2 cup (125 mL)	dry white wine
1 tbsp (15 mL)	chopped fresh dill

Pound scallopini, if necessary, to 1/8-inch (5-mm) thickness using a mallet or the edge of a sturdy saucer. In a shallow bowl, beat eggs with 2 tbsp (30 mL) water. Set aside. In a shallow bowl or deep plate, stir crumbs with lemon peel, salt and pepper. Dip each piece of scallopini in egg mixture. Shake off excess egg and coat on each side with crumb mixture. Lay in a single layer on a tray.

Preheat oven to 200°F (95°C). Heat oil in a non-stick skillet set over medium-high heat. When hot, add just enough meat to fill pan in a single layer. Cook, turning once, for 3 to 4 minutes or until golden. Add more oil if necessary. Transfer to a rimmed baking sheet and place in oven while cooking remaining meat.

Add butter to hot pan. Stir in capers and garlic. Cook, stirring, for 1 minute. Add the wine and bring to a boil. Cook, stirring often, for 3 minutes or until reduced to about 1/4 cup (50 mL). Stir in the dill. Arrange scallopini on a platter and drizzle sauce over top. Serve immediately.

Makes 2 to 3 servings. Recipe doubles easily.

Continued on next page...

Variation:

Fifteen-minute Veal Parmesan: Prepare scallopini as
directed above, omitting sauce ingredients. Substitute
1/3 cup (75 mL) grated Parmesan cheese for half the bread
crumbs. After placing browned scallopini into the oven,
heat 1 cup (250 mL) tomato or pasta sauce. Serve cooked
scallopini with sauce on the side.

Moroccan Spiced Pork Tenderloin

family favorite

fast fix

Exotic but approachable, this recipe is so yummy and fast it's likely to become a standby.

1	small onion, grated
¼ cup (50 mL)	orange juice
2 tbsp (30 mL)	brown sugar
½ tsp (2 mL)	finely grated lime peel
1 tbsp (15 mL)	lime juice
1	large clove garlic, minced
1 tbsp (15 mL)	finely grated ginger root
1 tsp (5 mL)	cinnamon
1 tsp (5 mL)	dried oregano leaves
½ tsp (2 mL)	ground coriander
¼ tsp (1 mL)	ground cardamom
¼ tsp (1 mL)	each salt and pepper
2	pork tenderloins, about 1 lb (500 g) each
2 tbsp (30 mL)	vegetable oil

Tip: This marinade is also great for chicken.

In a bowl, stir onion with orange juice, brown sugar, lime peel, lime juice, garlic, ginger, cinnamon, oregano, coriander, cardamom, salt and pepper.

Slice pork tenderloin into thin slices. Using a mallet or the bottom of a heavy mug, lightly pound to the thickness of a piece of scallopini. Place in bowl with marinade and toss to coat evenly.

Heat 2 tsp (10 mL) oil in a large non-stick frying pan set over medium-high heat. Working in batches and adding more oil as needed, add pork to pan. Cook, turning once, until golden brown on each side, about 5 minutes. Keep cooked meat warm in 200°F (95°C) oven.

Makes 4 to 6 servings.

Marmalade–Glazed Pork Tenderloin

Serve with mashed potatoes and steamed broccolini
or green beans.

1/2 cup (125 mL)	melted orange marmalade
1 tbsp (15 mL)	finely chopped fresh rosemary
1 tbsp (15 mL)	Dijon mustard
2	cloves garlic, minced
3/4 tsp (4 mL)	each salt and pepper
2	pork tenderloins, 1 lb (500 g) each

Stir marmalade with rosemary, mustard and garlic. Trim any
excess gristle or fat from tenderloins and toss to coat all
over with marmalade mixture. Let stand for 30 minutes, or
for up to 2 days, covered in refrigerator. Preheat oven to
400°F (200°C).

Sprinkle tenderloins evenly with salt and pepper and place
on a rimmed baking sheet, turning the thin part of the tail
up under the thicker part of the loin. Place tenderloins in
preheated oven and cook, basting liberally at least twice
with pan drippings, for about 25 minutes, or until an instant
read thermometer inserted into meat registers 165°F
(80°C). Let rest for 5 minutes before slicing into medallions.

Makes 4 servings.

Tip: Any of these marinated
pork tenderloin recipes is
suitable for grilling. Grill
over medium-high heat for
15 minutes, turning and
basting often.

Variations:

Maple-mustard: Replace marmalade with 1/4 cup (50 mL) maple syrup and increase mustard to 2 tbsp (30 mL). Substitute thyme for rosemary, if you like.

Lemon-tarragon: Omit marmalade, mustard and rosemary. Substitute 1 tbsp (15 mL) grated lemon peel, 2 tbsp (30 mL) lemon juice, 1 tbsp (15 mL) honey and 2 tsp (10 mL) finely chopped fresh tarragon.

Asian barbecue: Omit marmalade, mustard and rosemary. Combine 1/2 cup (125 mL) barbecue sauce, 2 tbsp (30 mL) soy sauce and 1 tbsp (15 mL) each finely grated ginger root and honey.

Cider-raisin: Omit marmalade and mustard. Substitute thyme for rosemary and combine in a blender with 1/2 cup (125 mL) apple cider or juice, 2 tbsp (30 mL) sultana raisins, 1 shallot or 1/2 small onion, chopped, and 1 clove garlic. Blend until smooth. Marinate and cook tenderloin as directed above.

pantry plus

make-ahead

Curried Lamb Kabobs with Chutney Sauce

These kabobs are equally tasty served over rice or wrapped in flat bread like a sandwich.

2 tbsp (30 mL)	olive oil
1 tbsp (15 mL)	mild Indian curry paste
2	cloves garlic, minced
1 (570 g) pkg	thawed frozen boneless lamb loins, about 1/2 lb
1/2 tsp (2 mL)	each salt and pepper
1/2 cup (125 mL)	plain yogurt
2 tbsp (30 mL)	mango chutney
1 tsp (5 mL)	ground cumin
dash	hot pepper sauce
10	fresh mint leaves
1	clove garlic, minced
	metal or wooden skewers

Stir olive oil with curry paste and half the garlic. Cut lamb into 1-inch (2.5-cm) cubes. Toss lamb to coat evenly in curry mixture. Cover tightly and refrigerate for 4 hours or up to 1 day.

Preheat grill or broiler. Thread 4 cubes of meat onto each metal or wooden skewer (if using wooden skewers, soak in water for 30 minutes to prevent scorching). Brush all over with any marinade remaining in bowl. Sprinkle evenly with salt and pepper.

Combine remaining garlic, yogurt, chutney and mint in a mini-chopper, blender or food processor and whirl until almost smooth.

Grill kabobs on a greased grill over medium-high heat,
turning occasionally, for about 10 minutes or until charred
on each side and medium-rare. Let rest for 5 minutes
before serving. Serve with chutney sauce on the side.

Variation:

Skewered lamb chops: Proceed as above but thread
2 lamb chops onto each skewer instead of 4 chunks of
loin. Reduce cooking time to 5 to 7 minutes.

fast but fancy

pantry plus

Basic Roasted Rack of Lamb

Rack of lamb is a very sophisticated yet quick dinner to prepare, making it ideal for weeknight or rushed entertaining.

3 tbsp (45 mL)	Dijon mustard
1 tbsp (15 mL)	chopped fresh rosemary or thyme
1 tsp (5 mL)	olive oil
3/4 tsp (2 mL)	each salt and pepper
2	cloves garlic, minced
2	racks of New Zealand lamb, about 1 lb (500 g) each

Preheat oven to 425°F (220°C).

Combine mustard with rosemary or thyme, olive oil, garlic, salt and pepper. Rub all over the fleshy side of frenched racks of lamb. Place lamb, bone side down, on a rack set over a rimmed baking sheet. Place in the center of preheated oven.

Roast for about 25 minutes or until internal temperature registers 140°F (60°C) on an instant read thermometer. If the outside of the meat is not browned, broil for 1 to 2 minutes. Let rest for 5 minutes. Place racks on a cutting board and turn bone side down. Using a heavy knife, slice between each set of bones to separate rack into chops.

Makes 4 servings.

Variations:

Pepper glazed: Replace Dijon mustard with 1/4 cup (50 mL) melted red pepper jelly.

Kasbah: Omit Dijon mustard and rosemary and increase olive oil to 2 tbsp (30 mL). Increase garlic to 4 cloves. Combine oil with garlic, 1/4 cup (50 mL) lightly packed fresh mint leaves, 2 tbsp (30 mL) lemon juice, 1 1/2 tsp (7 mL) ground pepper, 1 tsp (5 mL) each ground coriander and dried oregano and 1/2 tsp (2 mL) ground cloves in a food processor or mini-chopper. Blend until well combined. Rub mixture evenly over lamb and proceed as above.

Lamb chops: Use any of the above flavor combinations on lamb chops. To cook, place on an oiled, foil lined rimmed baking sheet. Preheat broiler and raise oven rack to about 4 inches (10 cm) below the broiler. Place pan in oven and broil chops, turning once, for 7 to 8 minutes or until cooked to medium rare.

Or, grill chops on a lightly greased grate over medium-high heat for 5 to 7 minutes.

Citrus–Tarragon Roasted Salmon

One of the pleasures of this easy recipe is that the salmon tastes good served hot or at room temperature.

1/4 cup (50 mL)	orange juice concentrate
1/4 cup (50 mL)	dry sherry
2 tbsp (30 mL)	fresh tarragon or 1 tsp (5 mL) dried
1 tbsp (15 mL)	butter, melted
1/2 tsp (2 mL)	each salt and pepper
1	clove garlic, minced
8	boneless, skinless center-cut salmon fillets, about 3 lbs (1.5 kg)

Stir orange juice concentrate with sherry, tarragon, butter, salt, pepper and garlic until well combined. Brush all over the fish. Cover and let stand in refrigerator for 1 hour or up to 4 hours.

Preheat oven to 425°F (220°C). Place fish on a buttered baking sheet. Brush evenly with the orange mixture in the marinating pan. Place on center rack of preheated oven and cook for 8 to 10 minutes or until flesh flakes easily with a fork but is still coral-colored in the center.

Makes 8 servings.

Niçoise Burgers

Quick, easy and hot, this pantry supper is a winner in summer or winter.

2	eggs
1/3 cup (75 mL)	dry bread crumbs
1 tbsp (15 mL)	mayonnaise
1 tsp (5 mL)	Dijon mustard
1	clove garlic, minced
1/4 cup (50 mL)	chopped black olives
1/4 tsp (1 mL)	pepper
1/4 tsp (1 mL)	anchovy paste
2 cans (6.5 oz/184 g each)	water-packed tuna
1	tomato, seeded and chopped
1 tbsp (15 mL)	vegetable oil
4	whole wheat kaiser rolls or hamburger buns
	alfalfa sprouts or lettuce
	mayonnaise (optional)

Beat eggs and mix in crumbs, mayonnaise, mustard, garlic, olives, pepper and anchovy paste. Drain tuna and flake into pieces using a fork.

Stir tuna and tomatoes into crumb mixture. Shape into four patties, each about 1/2 inch (1 cm) thick.

Heat a non-stick skillet over medium heat. Add oil and cook burgers, turning once, for 10 minutes or until golden brown. Place on buns and top with sprouts or lettuce. Serve with extra mayonnaise on the side, if you like.

Makes 4 servings.

pantry trick

fast fix

meatless

fast fix

fast but fancy

Roasted Sea Bass with Saffron-Citrus Glaze

Prepare this dish and enjoy restaurant-style elegance in less than 30 minutes!

Saffron-Citrus Glaze:

1½ cups (375 mL)	fish or light chicken broth
1 cup (250 mL)	orange juice
½ cup (125 mL)	vermouth or sherry
2 tsp (10 mL)	grated orange peel
½ tsp (2 mL)	saffron threads
2 tbsp (30 mL)	cold butter, cubed
½ tsp (2 mL)	salt
½ tsp (2 mL)	pepper

Fish:

2 tbsp (30 mL)	fresh bread crumbs
2 tbsp (30 mL)	almonds
1 tsp (5 mL)	grated orange peel
1 tsp (5 mL)	chopped fresh thyme
¼ tsp (1 mL)	each salt and pepper
2 tbsp (30 mL)	melted butter
8	farmed sea bass or halibut fillets, about 6 oz (150 g) each, 1 inch (2.5 cm) thick

Glaze:

Combine broth, orange juice, vermouth or sherry, orange peel and saffron in wide saucepan. Bring to boil and cook for about 15 minutes or until reduced to about 1 cup (250 mL). Reduce heat to low and slowly whisk in butter, cube by cube, salt and pepper. Keep sauce warm. Preheat oven to 450°F (230°C).

Combine bread crumbs, almonds, orange peel, thyme, salt and pepper in food processor. Process until almonds are the same size as crumbs.

Brush one side of each fillet with enough melted butter to coat. Press buttered side of fish into crumb mixture to coat evenly. Transfer to a lightly greased baking sheet and cook for 12 to 15 minutes in preheated oven or until flesh flakes easily with a fork and topping is evenly browned.

Transfer cooked fish to serving plates and spoon an equal amount of sauce around each piece.

Makes 8 servings.

healthier choice

fast but fancy

Black Bean–Ginger Poached Salmon

This aromatic dish is excellent as the centerpiece of a multi-course Asian dinner or served alone with rice for a delicious, low-fat weeknight meal.

2¹/₂ cups (625 mL)	water
2¹/₂ cups (625 mL)	fish or chicken broth or clam juice
¹/₂ cup (125 mL)	sake or medium sherry
¹/₄ cup (50 mL)	rinsed fermented black beans
¹/₃ cup (75 mL)	tamari
3 tbsp (45 mL)	hoisin sauce
2 tbsp (30 mL)	mirin
1 tbsp (15 mL)	brown sugar
1 tbsp (15 mL)	freshly grated ginger root
¹/₂ tsp (2 mL)	hot pepper sauce
2	cloves garlic, minced
6	skinless salmon fillets, about 6 oz (150 g) each
¹/₂ cup (125 mL)	julienned daikon or radish
6 to 8	chives

Tip: Daikon is a long, white Asian radish with a crisp, sweet flavor.

Bring water, broth, sake or sherry, black beans, tamari, hoisin, mirin, brown sugar, ginger, hot pepper sauce and garlic to a boil in a fish poacher or Dutch oven set over high heat; reduce heat and simmer for 10 minutes. Reduce heat until liquid is barely simmering.

Use a large, flat metal spatula or palette knife to place as many fillets as will fit into pan without being crowded. Place a lid just smaller than circumference of pan on top of fish to keep it submerged. Poach for 7 to 9 minutes or until fish is opaque on the outside but still coral-colored in the middle. Slide spatula lengthwise under each piece of fish and place in wide individual Japanese-style soup plates or pasta bowls. Cover and reserve. Repeat until all the fillets are cooked.

Increase heat to high and bring poaching liquid to a boil; add daikon and cook for 1 minute. Ladle a little poaching liquid over each piece of fish. Chop chives into 3/4-inch (2-cm) lengths and sprinkle into bowls.

Makes 6 servings.

fast but fancy

pantry plus

Asian Duck Breasts

You couldn't choose a more elegant main course or one that was any easier to prepare! Serve with rice and steamed baby bok choy for a lovely, yet straightforward meal.

1/4 cup (50 mL)	hoisin sauce
2 tbsp (30 mL)	soy sauce
2 tbsp (30 mL)	dry sherry
1 tbsp (15 mL)	sesame oil
1 tbsp (15 mL)	minced fresh ginger
1 tbsp (15 mL)	finely grated orange peel
1 tsp (5 mL)	pepper
4	boneless duck breasts, 8 oz (250 g) each or two, 16-oz (500-g) breasts
1/2 tsp (2 mL)	salt
2 tbsp (30 mL)	vegetable oil
1 tsp (5 mL)	liquid honey

Tips: If using larger duck breasts, extend oven-roasting time to 6 to 7 minutes.

Vacuum packaged duck breasts freeze well so feel free to stock up on them.

Stir hoisin sauce with soy sauce, sherry, sesame oil, ginger, orange peel and pepper. Remove duck breasts from package; pat dry and add to marinade, turning to coat. Let stand for 15 minutes or up to 4 hours.

Preheat oven to 400°F (200°C). Remove duck from marinade and pat skin side dry with a paper towel. Place skin side up on a plate. Sprinkle evenly with salt.

Heat oil in a heavy, ovenproof skillet set over medium-high heat. Add duck, skin side down, and cook for 2 minutes or until golden on the bottom. Turn and coat skin with marinade. Cook for 2 minutes. Turn again so that skin side is down and set skillet in oven. Roast for 3 to 4 minutes or until cooked to medium-rare, about 90°F (45°C) on an instant read thermometer.

Remove duck from oven and brush honey evenly over skin. Let rest on a platter or cutting board for 5 minutes before slicing lengthwise into long thin strips.

Makes 4 servings.

Weeknight Paella

A trendy use for leftover rice.

1 bottle (8 oz/237 mL)	clam juice
¼ tsp (1 mL)	saffron
1 tsp (5 mL)	vegetable oil
1	chorizo or spicy Italian sausage, sliced
1	red pepper, quartered and sliced
¼ cup (50 mL)	white wine
2 tbsp (30 mL)	tomato or pasta sauce
2	cloves garlic, minced
3 cups (750 mL)	cooked long grain rice
½ lb (250 g)	peeled, deveined raw shrimp, tails removed
½ cup (125 mL)	frozen peas, rinsed
2	green onions, thinly sliced
	salt and pepper
	lemon wedges

Tips: Chorizo sausage is available in specialty grocers and Spanish and Portuguese supermarkets.

If using frozen cleaned shrimp, rinse under cold running water until ice crystals disappear then drain well before cooking.

Pour clam juice into a measuring cup or heatproof bowl and heat in the microwave until steaming. Stir in saffron and reserve.

Heat vegetable oil in a deep, heavy skillet set over medium-high heat. Stir in sausage and cook, stirring often, until browned. Add peppers and cook, stirring often, for 3 to 5 minutes or until softened. Stir in wine, tomato or pasta sauce, garlic and clam juice mixture. Bring to a boil.

Stir in rice, shrimp, peas and green onions. Cook, tossing, until shrimp are bright pink and rice is heated through, about 2 minutes. Taste and adjust seasoning if necessary. Serve with a lemon wedge on the side.

Makes 4 servings.

fast but fancy

pantry plus

leftover wizard

meatless

leftover wizard

family favorite

Nasi Goreng

This Indonesian rice dinner favorite has family appeal and weeknight ease.

2 tbsp (30 mL)	vegetable oil
2	eggs
1 tsp (5 mL)	hot red pepper flakes
1/4 tsp (1 mL)	salt
1	onion, peeled and chopped
1	carrot, coarsely grated
2 tbsp (30 mL)	ketjap manis*
1 tsp (5 mL)	fish sauce
3	cloves garlic, minced
4 cups (1 L)	cooked long grain rice
1 cup (250 mL)	finely chopped English cucumber
1 tbsp (15 mL)	lime juice
3	green onions, thinly sliced

Heat half the oil in a non-stick skillet set over medium heat. Break the eggs into a small bowl and whisk in red pepper flakes and salt. Pour into pan and cook, covered, for 3 to 4 minutes or until firmly set. Using a spatula, roll up egg pinwheel-style and remove from pan. Cut into thin strips and reserve.

Add remaining oil, onion and carrot to pan. Cook, stirring often, for 5 minutes. Stir in ketjap manis, fish sauce and garlic. Stir in rice, cucumber, lime juice, green onions and reserved egg strips. Cook, tossing, until heated through.

Makes 4 servings.

*Ketjap manis is an Indonesian soy sauce that is often sold in delis and grocery stores that cater to a Dutch clientele. A good substitute for ketjap manis in this recipe is: 2 tbsp (30 mL) regular soy sauce mixed with 1/2 tsp (2 mL) molasses.

Twenty-Minute Linguine with Clam Sauce, page 121

Lime-Glazed Scallops on Creamy Wasabi
Fettucine, page 122

Caesar Salad Sandwich, page 132

Luau Rice, page 144

Twenty-Minute Linguine with Clam Sauce

Fool them all with this three-step sophisticate!

12 oz (375 g)	dry linguine
1 can (19 oz/540 mL)	Italian-style stewed tomatoes
1 can (14 oz/398 mL)	baby clams
1 tsp (5 mL)	balsamic vinegar
1/4 tsp (1 mL)	each salt and pepper
2 tbsp (30 mL)	finely chopped fresh basil (optional)
1/4 cup (50 mL)	grated Parmesan cheese

Cook pasta in a large pot of boiling salted water for 10 to 12 minutes or until al dente. Drain well.

Bring tomatoes to a boil in a deep skillet set over medium-high heat; cook, stirring and breaking up larger chunks, for 3 to 5 minutes or until slightly thickened. Drain and discard juices from clams then stir clams into pan with vinegar. Return to boil. Stir in basil (if using). Season to taste with salt and pepper.

Place drained noodles in a pasta bowl; add sauce and toss to combine. Sprinkle with Parmesan cheese and serve.

Makes 4 generous servings.

pantry trick

fast but fancy

family favorite

fast but fancy

pantry plus

Lime-Glazed Scallops on Creamy Wasabi Fettuccine

This rich dish is expensive to make but so inventive and delicious that it's sure to make a lasting impression.

12 oz (375 g)	dried fettuccine or tagliatelle
1/3 cup (75 mL)	pickled ginger
2 lbs (1 kg)	large sea scallops
1 tbsp (15 mL)	freshly grated lime peel
2	cloves garlic, minced
	salt and pepper
2 tbsp (30 mL)	vegetable oil
1 tbsp (15 mL)	wasabi powder
1 1/4 cups (300 mL)	35% cream
1/4 cup (50 mL)	butter
1 cup (250 mL)	grated Parmesan cheese (optional)
	chopped chives

Bring a large pot of salted water to a boil. Add pasta and cook until al dente, 10 to 12 minutes. Drain well. Chop 1/4 cup (50 mL) of the ginger and reserve.

Remove connective muscle (it looks like a little knob on the side of the scallop) from each scallop and discard. Pat dry. Toss scallops with lime peel, garlic and a little salt and pepper.

Heat vegetable oil in a large, heavy skillet set over medium-high heat. Add about one-third of the scallops to the pan and cook, without disturbing, for 2 minutes or until deep golden. They may stick at first but will then release as they become brown. Turn and cook for 2 minutes longer or until cooked through and deeply golden on the other side. Remove from pan and repeat as necessary to cook all of the remaining scallops.

Blend wasabi with 2 tbsp (30 mL) of cream to make a paste. Pour remaining cream into skillet used to cook the scallops. Add butter and bring to a boil. Reduce heat and whisk in wasabi paste, chopped ginger and Parmesan (if using). Add noodles and cooked scallops.

Toss to coat in sauce. Taste and adjust salt and pepper to taste. Transfer to pasta bowls and garnish with rosettes made from the remaining pickled ginger and chives.

Makes 6 servings.

pantry plus

fast fix

family favorite

Chicken and Vegetable Chow Mein

This is my take on a "classic" North American-style chow mein. Use whatever quick-cooking veggies you have on hand.

1 pkg (12oz/350 g)	fresh chow mein noodles
3/4 cup (175 mL)	chicken broth
1/3 cup (75 mL)	light soy sauce
3 tbsp (45 mL)	mirin or sherry
3 tbsp (45 mL)	oyster sauce
3 tbsp (45 mL)	hoisin sauce
4 tsp (20 mL)	cornstarch
2 tbsp (30 mL)	vegetable oil
2 tbsp (30 mL)	sesame oil
1	clove garlic, sliced
3/4 lb (375 g)	sliced, skinless, boneless chicken breasts
1	red pepper cut into long, thin strips
2 cups (500 mL)	chopped bok choy
1 cup (250 mL)	sliced snow peas

Loosen noodles. Immerse noodles in boiling water for 2 minutes. Drain well; fluff and reserve.

Whisk broth with soy sauce, mirin or sherry, oyster sauce, hoisin sauce and cornstarch in a small bowl or measuring cup. Reserve.

Heat oils in a wok or deep skillet set over high heat. Add garlic and cook, stirring, for 1 minute; remove garlic and discard. Add chicken strips and stir-fry for 3 to 4 minutes or until browned. Remove from pan and reserve. Stir in pepper and bok choy and stir-fry for 2 minutes. Stir in snow peas and stir-fry for 1 minute; add chicken.

Make a well in the center of the mixture by pushing vegetables up sides of pan. Stir cornstarch mixture vigorously and pour into well; cook, stirring, for 1 to 2 minutes or until sauce is lightly thickened.

Add noodles to wok and cook, tossing to combine noodles, vegetables and meat, for 2 to 3 minutes or until heated through.

Makes 6 servings.

Variations:

Pork or beef: Substitute equal amount of thinly sliced tender pork or beef for chicken.

Shrimp: Substitute 1 lb (500 g) small raw shrimp, shells and tails removed, for chicken. Reduce cooking time to 2 minutes or until pink.

fast but fancy

pantry plus

Easy Pad Thai

This version of the Thai classic can be prepared quickly, making it perfect for weeknight family suppers. Even though the ingredients may sound exotic, all of them are available in large chain grocery stores and most of these items keep for ages in the pantry.

8 oz (250 g)	medium width rice noodles
1/4 cup (50 mL)	vegetable oil
1/2 tsp (2 mL)	sambal oelek or hot sauce
1 1/2 cups (375 mL)	diced, extra firm tofu
1/4 lb (125 g)	ground pork
1	red pepper, chopped
3	cloves garlic, minced
2 tbsp (30 mL)	minced prawns in spice (optional)
1 tsp (5 mL)	freshly grated ginger root
1/3 cup (75 mL)	vegetable or chicken broth
3 tbsp (45 mL)	fish sauce
2 tbsp (30 mL)	granulated sugar
3 tbsp (45 mL)	ketchup
2 tbsp (30 mL)	lime juice
1/2 lb (250 g)	peeled, deveined raw shrimp
1 1/2 cups (375 mL)	bean sprouts
3	green onions, chopped
1/3 cup (75 mL)	fresh coriander leaves
1/3 cup (75 mL)	chopped roasted peanuts or cashews
	lime wedges

Place noodles in a large bowl; cover with boiling water and let stand for 5 minutes; drain and reserve.

Heat half the oil in a large wok or deep skillet with the sambal oelek or hot sauce over high heat until very hot.

Add the tofu and pork and stir-fry for 5 to 7 minutes or until well browned on every side. Remove from skillet and reserve. Add remaining oil and red peppers; stir-fry for 3 minutes or until peppers are starting to brown.

Stir in garlic, prawns (if using), ginger, broth, fish sauce, sugar, ketchup and lime juice; add shrimp and stir-fry for 2 minutes. Add noodles and tofu mixture and cook, tossing to combine, for 1 minute or until shrimp are pink all over.

Add sprouts and toss gently until mixed. Taste and adjust seasoning if necessary. Sprinkle with onions, coriander and peanuts or cashews. Turn onto a deep serving platter and serve garnished with lime wedges.

Makes 4 servings.

family favorite

fast fix

meatless

Pancakes for Supper

Pancakes are one of my favorite quick suppers—especially in the winter when I want a meal that will stick to my ribs.

Classic:

2 cups (500 mL)	all-purpose flour
1/4 cup (50 mL)	granulated sugar
4 tsp (20 mL)	baking powder
1/2 tsp (2 mL)	salt
2	eggs, lightly beaten
2 cups (500 mL)	milk
1 tsp (5 mL)	vanilla
1/4 cup (50 mL)	melted butter or vegetable oil

Heat a griddle or heavy skillet over medium-high heat. Preheat oven to 200°F (95°C). Whisk flour with sugar, baking powder and salt. Make a well in the dry ingredients and pour in eggs, milk, vanilla and butter or oil. Stir until well combined and almost smooth.

Grease preheated griddle or pan lightly and reduce heat to medium. Spoon batter onto griddle, using the back of the spoon to spread it into a circle. Cook for 1 to 2 minutes or until bubbles begin to form in batter. Turn and cook for 1 to 2 minutes longer or until golden. Transfer to oven until all pancakes are cooked.

Makes 4 servings.

Tip: Layer leftover pancakes between slices of waxed paper and freeze. Warm in the toaster to serve later.

Variations:

Blueberry: Thaw 3/4 cup (175 mL) frozen blueberries and drain well. Sprinkle a few berries over pancake batter just after adding to griddle. Alternatively, fold the same amount of fresh wild or cultivated berries into batter.

Bacon: Stir 1/2 cup (125 mL) very finely chopped cooked bacon or ham into batter.

Cornmeal Pancakes

Perfect for pancake suppers or for weekend brunch.

1¹/₂ cups (375 mL)	cornmeal
¹/₂ cup (125 mL)	all-purpose flour
1 tsp (5 mL)	baking powder
¹/₂ tsp (2 mL)	baking soda
¹/₂ tsp (2 mL)	salt
2 cups (500 mL)	buttermilk or sour milk
2 tbsp (30 mL)	granulated sugar
2 tbsp (30 mL)	vegetable oil
1	egg, beaten
	maple syrup

Mix cornmeal with flour, baking powder, baking soda and salt in a medium bowl. Combine buttermilk or sour cream with sugar, vegetable oil and egg. Add the cornmeal mixture and stir until the ingredients are just blended. Let stand for 10 minutes.

Heat a non-stick griddle or large heavy skillet over medium-high heat. When pan is hot grease lightly. Pour about 1/4 cup (50 mL) batter onto pan to make each pancake. Cook for 2 to 3 minutes or until bottoms are golden and bubbles start to form in batter. Turn and cook for 2 minutes longer. Serve with maple syrup on the side.

Makes 6 servings.

Tip: No buttermilk on hand? See page 17 for directions on how to make sour milk yourself.

Variation:

Santa Fe Pancakes: Reduce sugar to 1 tbsp (15 mL) and add 1¹/₂ tsp (7 mL) chili powder. Stir ¹/₂ cup (125 mL) cooked corn kernels into batter. Serve with salsa and sour cream.

family favorite

fast fix

meatless

meatless

pantry plus

make-ahead

California Stuffed Baked Potatoes

These stuffed potatoes are hearty vegetarian entrées.

2	large baking potatoes, about 4 lbs (2 kg)
1 tbsp (15 mL)	butter
1 cup (250 mL)	finely chopped shiitake mushrooms, about 6 oz (175 g)
1 tsp (5 mL)	lemon peel
2 tsp (10 mL)	balsamic vinegar or lemon juice
1/4 tsp (1 mL)	each salt and pepper
1/3 cup (75 mL)	hot milk
1 roll (113 g)	creamy goat cheese
1/4 cup (50 mL)	finely chopped oil-packed sun-dried tomatoes, blotted dry
2 tsp (10 mL)	basil pesto or finely chopped fresh basil

Scrub potatoes then pierce with a knife or skewer. Bake in microwave on high for 5 minutes. Turn and cool, adding 2 to 3 minutes longer for each potato in microwave, or cook until fork tender. Or, bake potatoes in a preheated 400°F (200°C) oven for about 45 minutes. Remove from oven and cool until able to handle.

Melt the butter in a skillet set over medium-high heat. Add mushrooms and cook for 5 minutes or until golden; drain off any butter standing in pan and stir in lemon peel and balsamic vinegar or lemon juice. Season with salt and pepper and reserve.

Cut potatoes in half lengthwise. Using a spoon, scoop out insides of potatoes leaving a layer of potato next to the skin thick enough to maintain the potato shape. Mash scooped-out potatoes with a hand-held masher or a potato ricer.

Stir milk and goat cheese into mashed potatoes and whip with an electric mixer until fluffy. Using a spatula, fold in shiitake mixture, sun-dried tomatoes and pesto or fresh basil. Taste and adjust seasoning if necessary. Mound whipped potato mixture back into skins. Cover and reserve. Preheat oven to 350°F (180°C).

Place potatoes in a baking pan and bake, covered, in oven for 30 to 45 minutes or until hot in the center. Or, microwave, covered, on high for 2 minutes each. Remove cover and broil for 2 to 3 minutes or until golden.

Makes 4 servings.

Variations:

Lemon-asparagus: Omit mushrooms, sun-dried tomatoes and pesto. Substitute 1/2 tsp (2 mL) more lemon juice for balsamic vinegar. Stir 2 tsp (10 mL) finely grated lemon peel and 1 cup (250 mL) blanched asparagus tips and stems, cut into 1-inch (5-cm) lengths, into potato mixture.

Broccoli-cheddar: Omit mushrooms and sun-dried tomatoes. Stir in 11/2 cups (375 mL) small blanched broccoli florets. Sprinkle 1/4 cup (50 mL) shredded cheddar cheese over stuffed potatoes before baking.

fast fix

pantry trick

Caesar Salad Sandwich

Turning a classic salad into a sandwich creates a meal that is sure to be a hit.

2	thick slices sourdough or other crusty bread
2 tbsp (30 mL)	Safe Caesar Dressing (see page 62)
2	romaine lettuce leaves
1 tbsp (15 mL)	Parmesan cheese shards or grated Parmesan cheese
2	strips crispy cooked bacon or 3 tbsp (45 mL) pre-cooked real bacon bits or pieces

Toast bread lightly under the broiler or on the grill. Spread dressing evenly over each slice and stack romaine leaves, trimming to fit, on top of one slice. Lay bacon on top and sprinkle with Parmesan. Cover with second piece of toasted bread, dressing side down. Slice in half and serve.

Makes 1 serving.

Tips: Use ready cooked bacon for the speediest preparation.

To make sandwiches for a crowd, slice a long Italian-style loaf of bread in half lengthwise. Dress like one big sandwich and then slice into individual servings.

Grilled Ham and Cheese Club

Uniting lunchtime favorites, like grilled cheese and club sandwiches, this new approach uses items many people routinely keep on hand.

3	small wheat flour tortillas or slices whole wheat bread
1/3 cup (75 mL)	grated cheddar cheese
3	tomato slices
1 tbsp (15 mL)	mango chutney or Branston pickle
1	thick slice Black Forest ham, about 2 oz (60 g)
1 tsp (5 mL)	butter

Spread tortillas or bread on countertop. Spread chutney evenly over top. Sprinkle some of the cheese evenly over chutney and top with slice of ham. Sprinkle with a little more cheese.

Top with another tortilla and sprinkle over a little more cheese. Lay tomato slices on top and add salt and pepper to taste. Sprinkle over remaining cheese. Stack last tortilla, chutney side down, on top. Cut in half.

Tip: Try grilling this sandwich on the barbecue for a deeper flavor and great-looking grill marks.

Melt butter in a non-stick skillet set over medium heat. Place stacked sandwich halves in pan next to one another. Cook for about 3 minutes, turning with tongs or an egg lifter. Cook for 2 minutes longer or until nicely toasted on each side and cheese has melted. Slice into triangles.

Makes 1 serving.

meatless

pantry plus

fast fix

Ambleside Beach Veggie Delight

Full flavored and colorful, this hearty vegetarian sandwich is great served with a tall glass of iced tea and a sunset.

2	slices multigrain or other bread
1 tbsp (15 mL)	basil pesto
3 or 4	arugula or other lettuce leaves
3	slices roasted red or yellow pepper
1 tsp (5 mL)	balsamic vinegar
2	slices Muenster cheese

Lay bread slices on countertop. Spread pesto evenly over one side of each slice. Top one slice with arugula. Pat peppers dry and stack on top. Drizzle over vinegar and top with cheese. Crown with second slice of bread, pesto side down. Slice in half and serve.

Makes 1 serving.

Side Dishes

Three Pantry Pasta Sauces

meatless

Although I recommend never running out of tomato sauce or canned tomatoes, sometimes it's hard to face the same old spaghetti with red sauce. For such occasions, here are three fast easy ways for dressing a noodle for dinner.

fast fix

Each of these sauces will coat 6 cups (1.5 L) of cooked pasta or about 12 oz (375 g) dry pasta.

1. Lemon and Parmesan Butter Sauce

family favorite

Fresh, fast and scrumptious, my son Oliver often requests this for his supper.

1/3 cup (75 mL)	butter
1/4 cup (50 mL)	grated Parmesan cheese (approx)
1 tbsp (15 mL)	finely grated lemon or lime peel
1/2 tsp (2 mL)	coarsely ground pepper
	salt

Melt butter. Stir in Parmesan, citrus peel and pepper. Toss with noodles. Taste and add salt to taste. Serve with additional cheese at the table.

Makes 4 to 6 servings.

Variation:

Lemon-lime: Substitute 1 1/2 tsp (7 mL) each finely grated lemon and lime peel for lemon peel.

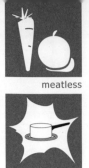

meatless

fast fix

2. Blender Roasted Red Pepper Sauce

Pull this pantry sauce out of the cupboard to perk up pasta.

1 can or jar (400 g)	roasted red peppers, about 5 peppers
2 tbsp (30 mL)	extra virgin olive oil
1	clove garlic
1 tbsp (15 mL)	balsamic vinegar
1/4 cup (50 mL)	lightly packed fresh basil leaves or 2 tbsp (30 mL) pesto
	grated Parmesan cheese

Drain peppers and combine in a blender with oil, garlic, vinegar and basil or pesto. Blend until smooth, adding up to 1/4 cup (50 mL) water to make a smooth sauce as necessary.

Bring to a boil and toss with pasta. Sprinkle with Parmesan cheese and serve.

Makes 4 to 6 servings.

Tip: I recommend that you use better quality balsamic vinegar for optimum taste but if vinegar is very tart, reduce to 2 tsp (10 mL), or add a pinch of sugar to sauce if too tangy.

3. Aglio e Olio Sauce

Although I wouldn't recommend eating this dish before a hot date, it is wonderful almost any other time.

1/2 cup (125 mL)	extra virgin olive oil
6	cloves garlic, minced
1 tsp (5 mL)	salt
1/2 tsp (2 mL)	hot pepper flakes
1/4 cup (50 mL)	chopped fresh parsley, basil or coriander
	pepper

Heat olive oil in a skillet set over low heat. Cook garlic, stirring often, with salt and hot pepper flakes for about 10 minutes or until garlic is just slightly golden. Stir in herbs and toss with cooked noodles. Season with pepper to taste.

Makes 4 to 6 servings.

Variation:

Caper and olive: Stir 1/4 cup (50 mL) chopped, pitted kalamata or other black olives, 2 tbsp (30 mL) drained capers and 1 tsp (5 mL) finely grated lemon peel into lightly browned garlic. Cook, stirring, until heated through. Proceed as directed above.

Laissez Faire Risotto

Although the creamiest risotto is achieved by constantly stirring and slowly cooking it over low heat, this microwave version produces an acceptable alternative in half the time.

2 tbsp (30 mL)	butter
1	onion, peeled and chopped
1	clove garlic, minced
1/4 tsp (1 mL)	each salt and pepper
1 cup (250 mL)	arborio rice
3 cups (750 mL)	chicken broth
1/2 cup (125 mL)	white wine or additional chicken broth
1/2 cup (125 mL)	dried mushrooms, such as porcini
1 tsp (5 mL)	dried thyme leaves
1 tsp (5 mL)	grated lemon peel (optional)
1 cup (250 mL)	broccolini chunks or rapini
1/2 cup (125 mL)	freshly grated Parmesan cheese

Combine butter, onion, garlic, salt and pepper in a large microwaveable bowl. Cover tightly with plastic wrap; make a vent hole and cook on high power for 1 minute or until onion has softened.

Stir in rice, broth, wine, mushrooms, thyme, and lemon peel (if using). Cover and cook on high for 5 minutes. Stir well; cover and cook for 5 minutes longer. Repeat.

Add broccolini or rapini and cook for 1 to 2 minutes longer or until rice is al dente. Stir in cheese and let stand for 3 to 5 minutes. Taste and adjust seasoning if necessary.

Makes 4 to 6 servings.

Variations:

Squash: Omit mushrooms and broccolini. Add 1 1/2 cups (375 mL) diced peeled winter squash with rice.

Beet: Omit mushrooms and broccolini. Drain 1 can (14 oz/398 mL) cooked beets and dice finely. Add to rice mixture for last 5 minutes of cooking. Stir in 1 tbsp (15 mL) chopped fresh dill or 1 tsp (5 mL) dried dill.

Caramelized onion: Up to 2 days ahead, prepare onions as indicated on page 165. Omit cooking onion from original recipe and proceed as directed above.

Risotto cakes: Stir 1 beaten egg into each 2 cups of left-over risotto. Shape mixture into patties and reserve, tightly wrapped, in the refrigerator. To cook, heat 1 tbsp (15 mL) each of butter and cooking oil in a skillet set over medium-high heat. Add patties and cook, turning once, for about 3 minutes per side or until crisp and golden.

Risotto pie: Increase Parmesan cheese to 1 cup (250 mL). Beat 2 eggs and stir into cooked risotto. Press mixture into a greased 9-inch (23-cm) pie plate. (Can be prepared to this point, covered and reserved for up to 2 days in refrigerator.) Preheat oven to 350°F (180°C). Bake in preheated oven for 30 to 35 minutes or until golden and set in the center.

meatless

family favorite

fast fix

Gourmet Skillet Mac and Cheese

Almost as fast as the packaged stuff but infinitely better tasting. Feel free to mix and match the cheese and veggies for things you have on hand.

2 cups (500 mL)	dry elbow macaroni or other short pasta
2 tbsp (30 mL)	butter
2	onions, peeled and chopped
1	zucchini, halved and thinly sliced
1/2 tsp (2 mL)	dried thyme
1 tbsp (15 mL)	all-purpose flour
3/4 cup (175 mL)	milk
3 tbsp (45 mL)	finely chopped sun-dried tomatoes
3/4 tsp (4 mL)	pepper
1/2 tsp (2 mL)	salt
1	clove garlic, minced
2 cups (500 mL)	shredded Italian blend cheese (or 11/2 cups/375 mL shredded mozzarella and 1/2 cup/125 mL grated Parmesan cheese)
1 tbsp (15 mL)	chopped fresh parsley (optional)

Tip: If necessary, wrap the plastic handle of the skillet with foil to protect it from heat under the broiler.

Cook macaroni for 8 to 10 minutes, or until tender, in a large pot of boiling salted water. Drain well and reserve.

Melt half the butter in an ovenproof deep skillet or shallow saucepan set over medium heat. Add onion and cook for 5 minutes. Add zucchini and thyme; cook for 4 to 5 minutes or until softened and browned. Remove from pan.

Melt remaining butter in skillet and sprinkle in flour. Cook, stirring, for 1 to 2 minutes. Stirring constantly, add milk a little at a time until well combined. Stir in sun-dried tomatoes, pepper, salt and garlic. Cook, stirring, until mixture comes to a boil.

Add 1 cup (250 mL) of cheese, a little at a time, stirring constantly until sauce is smooth. Stir in zucchini mixture and noodles. Sprinkle remaining cheese and parsley (if using) over top. Place under the broiler for 2 to 3 minutes or until cheese is brown and bubbly. Makes 4 generous servings.

Variations:

Broccoli: Substitute broccoli for the zucchini, adding broccoli to pasta cooking water 4 minutes after it starts boiling, and cheddar for the mozzarella. Omit sun-dried tomatoes.

Tex-Mex: Omit sun-dried tomatoes and zucchini. Add 1 tsp (5 mL) chili powder with flour and substitute Monterey Jack or cheddar for mozzarella, and oregano for thyme. Stir in chopped tomato and green onion just before broiling.

Mushroom and onion: Omit zucchini, sun-dried tomatoes and thyme. Add 2 cups (500 mL) sautéed mushrooms and onions and replace mozzarella with Gruyère.

leftover wizard

fast fix

Luau Rice

This yummy dish can be served hot or at room temperature.

1/3 cup (75 mL)	chicken or vegetable broth
1 tbsp (15 mL)	oyster sauce
1 tbsp (15 mL)	fish sauce
1 tbsp (15 mL)	mirin
2 tbsp (30 mL)	tamari (or light soy sauce)
2 tbsp (30 mL)	toasted sesame oil
1 tsp (5 mL)	brown sugar
1	clove garlic, minced
2 tbsp (30 mL)	vegetable oil
1/2 tsp (2 mL)	hot pepper flakes
1	small onion, peeled, halved and sliced
1/2	each red and yellow pepper, chopped
1 cup (250 mL)	sliced snow peas
2 cups (500 mL)	cooked basmati rice
1 cup (250 mL)	finely diced, peeled mango
2	green onions, chopped

Whisk broth with oyster sauce, fish sauce, mirin, tamari, sesame oil, sugar and garlic; reserve.

Heat oil in wok or deep skillet set over medium-high heat; add hot pepper flakes and cook for 1 minute or until fragrant. Stir in onion and stir-fry for 5 minutes or until softened and turning brown. Increase heat to high and add peppers; cook, stirring occasionally, for 3 minutes or until they begin to brown.

Add snow peas and reserved liquid mixture; boil for 2 minutes or until liquid is reduced and syrupy. Add rice, mango and green onions and cook, tossing, for 3 minutes or until heated through.

Makes 6 to 8 servings.

Cheesy Polenta Surprise, page 150

Maple-Glazed Carrots, page 161

Tuscan Green Bean Salad, page 162

Citrus Compote, page 170

Lemon-Herb Potato Pancakes

fast fix

leftover wizard

What a great way to reinvent leftover mashed potatoes!

1 cup (250 mL)	cooked mashed potatoes
1/2	small onion, peeled and finely chopped
1	egg, beaten
2 tbsp (30 mL)	crumbled feta cheese
1 tbsp (15 mL)	chopped fresh mint, oregano or thyme
1/2 tsp (2 mL)	grated lemon peel
1/4 tsp (1 mL)	pepper
pinch	salt
1 tbsp (15 mL)	vegetable oil
1 tbsp (15 mL)	lemon juice

Break apart potatoes using a fork. Stir onions with eggs, feta, herbs, lemon peel, pepper and salt. Pour over potato mixture and stir until well combined. Shape into patties each about 3 inches (8 cm) wide.

Heat oil in a skillet or griddle set over medium-high heat. Add patties to pan and cook, turning halfway through, for 5 minutes or until golden brown and crisp. Sprinkle with lemon juice and serve as a side dish.

Makes 4 servings.

Tip: Great served with a dollop of sour cream or yogurt.

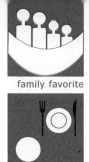

family favorite

pantry trick

Do The Mash—Basic Mashed Potatoes

Memorize this one. It will come in handy later.

4	potatoes, about 2 lbs (1 kg)
2 tbsp (30 mL)	butter
1/2 cup (125 mL)	warmed milk
1/4 tsp (1 mL)	each salt and pepper

Cook potatoes, partially covered, for 20 minutes in a large pot of boiling salted water; drain well and return pan to heat for 30 seconds or until bottom of pan is dry. Mash with a hand-held masher or a potato ricer.

Beat in butter, warm milk, salt and pepper. Taste and adjust seasonings if necessary.

Makes 4 servings.

Variations:

Wasabi: Stir in 3/4 tsp (4 mL) to 1 tsp (5 mL) wasabi paste or 11/2 tsp (7 mL) to 2 tsp (10 mL) prepared horseradish.

Roasted garlic: As potatoes boil, sauté 3 cloves of garlic until golden in a small skillet set over medium-high heat. Add just enough chicken broth or water to fill the bottom of the pan. Cook garlic, stirring and turning until all the liquid is evaporated and the garlic is soft. Mash with a fork and stir into potatoes along with butter and milk.

Cheddar: Stir 1/2 cup (125 mL) finely shredded sharp cheddar cheese into hot potatoes as you mash.

Creamy Mashed Potatoes with Shiitake and Bacon

Gourmet spuds can save any dinner from being a dud.

family favorite

fast but fancy

4	large potatoes, peeled and cut in chunks, about 2 lbs (1 kg)
2 tbsp (30 mL)	butter
1/2 cup (125 mL)	finely chopped bacon, about 6 oz (175 g)
1 cup (250 mL)	finely chopped shiitake mushrooms (about 6 oz/175 g)
1/2 cup (125 mL)	hot buttermilk
1/4 tsp (1 mL)	each salt and pepper

Cook potatoes, partially covered, for 20 minutes in a large pot of boiling, salted water; drain well and return pan to heat for 30 seconds or until bottom of pan is dry. Mash with a hand-held masher or a potato ricer.

Melt 1 tsp (5 mL) of the butter in a skillet set over medium-high heat. Add bacon and cook, stirring often, for 2 minutes or until it begins to brown. Stir in mushrooms and continue to cook for 5 minutes or until golden; drain off excess fat. Season with salt and pepper and reserve. (Can be prepared to this point, covered and refrigerated up to 2 days ahead.)

Stir remaining butter and buttermilk into potatoes and whip with an electric mixer on medium speed until fluffy. Using a spatula, fold in shiitake mixture. Taste and adjust seasoning if necessary.

Makes 4 servings.

Tip: Substitute 1/2 cup (125 mL) cooked bacon pieces for raw bacon. Cook mushrooms in butter and add bacon for last 30 seconds of cooking to combine flavors.

family favorite

fast but fancy

Red Potato Galettes

Tarragon highlights the delicious flavor of new spring potatoes in this impressive, easy recipe.

3 tbsp (45 mL)	butter
2 tbsp (30 mL)	finely chopped fresh tarragon
1/4 tsp (1 mL)	each salt and pepper
1/4 tsp (1 mL)	ground nutmeg
3	red new potatoes
1	small onion
1/2 cup (125 mL)	finely shredded Gruyère cheese

Melt butter and stir in tarragon, salt, pepper and nutmeg. Reserve. Wash potatoes and pat dry. Using a mandoline, food processor or very sharp chef's knife, thinly slice potatoes into disks. Slice onion into very thin rings. Toss potatoes and onions with butter mixture until evenly coated. Preheat oven to 375°F (190°C).

Line a rimmed baking sheet with parchment paper. Arrange potatoes and onions in overlapping, concentric rings, sprinkling cheese between each layer to make 6 equal round potato nests, each made of 3 layers of potato and 2 layers of onion. Top each galette evenly with shredded cheese.

Bake in preheated oven for 30 minutes or until crisp and golden around the edges and cooked through in the center. Let rest for 5 minutes before serving. Transfer to heated dinner plates using a metal spatula or cake lifter. (Can be made up to 2 hours ahead and reheated for 5 to 10 minutes in the oven just before serving.)

Makes 6 servings.

Variations:

Santa Fe: Omit tarragon and nutmeg. Combine 1 tsp (5 mL) chili powder and 1 tsp (5 mL) grated lime peel. Stir with melted butter, salt and pepper. Substitute cheddar or Monterey Jack for Gruyère.

Tuscan: Omit nutmeg. Substitute basil for tarragon. Add 1 tsp (5 mL) balsamic vinegar to butter mixture and replace Gruyère with shredded Parmesan cheese.

Faux scalloped potatoes: No time to shape galettes? Spread onions and potatoes evenly on a rimmed baking sheet. Sprinkle with cheese and bake as directed above.

fast but fancy

meatless

Cheesy Polenta Surprise

Serve this dish on its own just before the main course so that no one is too full to savor it.

	salted butter
1/3 cup (75 mL)	mascarpone cheese
1/2 tsp (2 mL)	finely grated lemon peel (optional)
6 cups (1.5 L)	chicken or vegetable broth
1 1/2 cups (375 mL)	fine cornmeal
1/3 cup (75 mL)	finely grated Parmesan cheese
1/2 tsp (2 mL)	each salt and pepper

Coat four serving plates thinly and evenly with butter. Stir mascarpone with lemon peel (if using) until smooth and combined. Roll into 4 equal balls. Press each ball onto center of each plate. Place in refrigerator or freezer.

Heat broth in a saucepan until boiling. Reduce heat to medium-low. Stirring constantly, add cornmeal to pan in a slow, steady stream. Stir until thickened, from 3 to 5 minutes. Reduce heat to low and cook, stirring often, for 15 minutes or until polenta is creamy and very thick. Stir in Parmesan, salt and pepper. Taste and adjust seasoning if necessary.

Spoon polenta over cold mascarpone and serve immediately.

Makes 4 servings.

Fifteen-Minute Orzo Pilaf

pantry trick

fast fix

Lighter than rice and quicker to prepare, orzo adds variety to weeknight meals.

1 tsp (5 mL)	butter
1 tsp (5 mL)	cinnamon
1 cup (250 mL)	dried orzo
1 1/2 cups (375 mL)	vegetable or chicken broth
1 tsp (5 mL)	finely grated orange peel
1/2 cup (125 mL)	orange juice
1/4 cup (50 mL)	chopped dried apricots, dates or raisins
1	green onion, chopped
	salt and pepper

Melt butter in a saucepan set over medium heat. Add cinnamon and cook, stirring, for 1 minute. Stir in orzo, broth and orange juice. Bring to a boil. Reduce heat to low and simmer gently for about 5 minutes or until liquid is almost completely absorbed.

Stir in dried fruit and orange peel. Cook for 2 to 3 minutes longer or until orzo is tender and liquid is completely absorbed. Fluff with a fork. Stir in green onion. Taste and adjust seasoning if necessary.

Makes 2 to 3 servings.

Variations:

Saffron-tomato: Substitute tomato sauce for orange juice. Omit cinnamon, orange peel, apricots and nuts. Stir 1/4 tsp (1 mL) saffron into juice before adding to orzo.

Curried: Omit cinnamon and substitute lime peel for orange peel. Stir 1 tsp (5 mL) mild Indian curry paste into broth before adding to orzo.

fast but fancy

make-ahead

Sweet Potato Timbales

Reinvent leftover vegetables for your next dinner party
or Sunday dinner.

4 cups (1 L)	puréed cooked sweet potato, about 2 potatoes
2 tbsp (30 mL)	chopped fresh coriander
1 tsp (5 mL)	lime or lemon juice
1 tsp (5 mL)	salt
1/2 tsp (2 mL)	pepper
6	egg whites, about 3/4 cup (175 mL)
1/2 cup (125 mL)	35% whipping cream
	coriander sprigs
	sour cream (optional)

Preheat oven to 350°F (180°C). Place sweet potatoes,
coriander, lime juice, salt and pepper in blender or food
processor; purée until very smooth. Add egg whites; pour in
cream and blend until well combined.

Divide potato mixture equally among six 1/2-cup (125-mL)
ramekins or custard cups. Place ramekins in baking pan;
pour in enough boiling water to come halfway up the sides
of the dishes. Cover with foil and make a few vent holes
in top.

Bake in oven for about 40 minutes or until a tester comes
out clean when inserted into center of a timbale. Rest for
2 to 3 minutes; run knife around edge of each dish and turn
timbales out onto warmed plates. Garnish each timbale with
a sprig of coriander and a dollop of sour cream (if using).

Makes 6 servings.

Variations:

Carrot: Substitute carrots for sweet potato; reduce coriander to 2 tsp (10 mL) and add 1 tsp (5 mL) minced ginger.

Mint and pea: Substitute peas for sweet potatoes. Cook peas in water mixed with 2 tsp (10 mL) salt to ensure color remains vibrant. Replace coriander with fresh mint or 1 tsp (5 mL) dried mint and omit lemon juice.

Parsnip and lemon: Substitute parsnips for sweet potato and thyme for coriander. Add 2 tsp (10 mL) finely grated lemon peel and increase lemon juice to 1 tbsp (15 mL).

pantry plus

fast fix

make-ahead

Balsamic-Orange Couscous

Don't forget to stock up on couscous. It is a mealtime lifesaver that can turn leftovers into a one-dish dinner in less than 10 minutes.

2 cups (500 mL)	instant regular or whole wheat couscous
1 3/4 cups (425 mL)	water
1 cup (250 mL)	orange juice
2	stalks celery, finely chopped
1	red pepper, quartered and thinly sliced
2	green onions, thinly sliced on the bias
1/4 cup (50 mL)	balsamic vinegar
1 tsp (5 mL)	finely grated orange peel
1	clove garlic, minced
1/2 tsp (2 mL)	each salt and pepper
1/2 cup (125 mL)	extra virgin olive oil

Place couscous in a large bowl. Combine water and juice in a small saucepan. Bring to a boil. Pour water mixture over couscous. Cover tightly and let stand for 5 minutes. Fluff with a fork and let cool for 10 minutes. Meanwhile, prepare vegetables and add to couscous mixture.

Stir balsamic vinegar with orange peel, garlic, salt and pepper in a small bowl. Whisk in olive oil then drizzle over couscous mixture. Toss to combine. Taste and adjust seasoning just before serving, if necessary. If making ahead, taste just before serving and add extra olive oil and balsamic vinegar if necessary.

Makes 12 servings.

Variations:

Pesto: Substitute vegetable or chicken broth for water and orange juice. Add 2 tbsp (30 mL) pesto to broth before mixing with couscous. Omit orange peel. Reduce balsamic vinegar to 1 tbsp (15 mL).

Tomato-herb: Substitute tomato juice for orange juice. Omit orange peel and reduce balsamic vinegar to 2 tbsp (30 mL). Stir in 1/4 cup (50 mL) chopped fresh basil or parsley.

fast but fancy

pantry trick

Cardamom-Scented Rutabaga Purée

What can I say, they're rutabagas. The French love 'em (especially with duck), my mom loves 'em and you will too once you taste this version, heady with the exotic flavor of cardamom.

1	rutabaga, about 2 lbs (1 kg)
2 tbsp (30 mL)	butter
2 tbsp (30 mL)	honey
1/4 tsp (1 mL)	ground cardamom
1/2 cup (125 mL)	warmed milk
1/2 tsp (2 mL)	each salt and pepper

Quarter rutabaga, peel and dice into large cubes. Place in a large saucepan. Cover with cold, salted water and bring to boil. Reduce heat and simmer for 25 to 30 minutes or until fork tender.

Drain well and transfer to a food processor. Add butter, honey and cardamom; process until smooth. With motor running, gradually pour in milk. Blend in salt and pepper. Continue to process until mixture is light and creamy. Taste and adjust seasonings if necessary. Can be reheated in microwave.

Makes 4 servings.

Carrot and Parsnip Smash

Jazz up winter veggies easily.

1 lb (500 g)	carrots
1 lb (500 g)	parsnips
1 tbsp (15 mL)	butter
1/2 cup (125 mL)	warmed milk
1 tbsp (15 mL)	chopped fresh thyme (optional)
1/2 tsp (2 mL)	each salt and pepper
1/2 tsp (2 mL)	ground nutmeg

Peel carrots and parsnips. Chop into chunks. (You should have about 8 cups/2 L combined). Place in a saucepan and cover with salted water. Bring to a boil. Reduce heat and simmer, partially covered, for 15 minutes or until very tender.

Drain well and mash in butter and milk until well combined but texture is still coarse. Stir in thyme (if using), salt, pepper and nutmeg. Taste and adjust seasonings if necessary.

Makes 6 servings.

pantry plus

fast but fancy

South Seas Mash

Another smashing idea for tubers!

2	large sweet potatoes, about 2 lbs (1 kg) in total
1/2 cup (125 mL)	coconut milk
1 tsp (5 mL)	grated lime peel
1 tbsp (15 mL)	lime juice
3/4 tsp (4 mL)	each salt and pepper
dash	hot pepper sauce
1/4 cup (50 mL)	chopped fresh coriander

Peel potatoes and chop into chunks. Place in a saucepan of salted water and bring to a boil over high heat. Reduce heat and simmer for 10 minutes or until fork tender.

Drain well and return to heat to dry. Mash in coconut milk, lime peel, lime juice, salt, pepper and hot sauce. Beat until very smooth. Stir in coriander. Taste and adjust seasonings if necessary.

Makes 4 to 6 servings.

Coriander-Scented Bok Choy

fast but fancy

healthier choice

This vegetable side dish is subtle yet sophisticated.

3/4 tsp (4 mL)	ground coriander seed
2 cups (500 mL)	chicken or vegetable broth
1 tbsp (15 mL)	lemon juice
3	cloves garlic, minced
1/4 tsp (1 mL)	each salt and pepper
1	bay leaf
8	baby bok choy
1/2 tsp (2 mL)	finely grated lemon peel

Toast coriander in a wide saucepan or Dutch oven set over medium heat for 1 minute or until fragrant. Stir in broth, lemon juice, garlic, salt, pepper and bay leaf. Bring to boil and remove from heat; cover and let stand for 10 minutes.

Wash bok choy under running water to remove any grit. Tear off any tough outer leaves. Add to broth and return to boil.

Tip: If using canned or reconstituted broth, omit salt.

Reduce heat and simmer, covered, for about 10 minutes or until tender; remove bok choy from pot and place on serving dish; tent with foil. (Can be made ahead to this point, cooled and refrigerated for up to 1 day. Reheat bok choy in cooking liquid and then proceed as specified below.) Bring broth mixture to a rolling boil. Simmer for 7 to 8 minutes or until reduced to about 1/4 cup (50 mL). Remove bay leaf and pour over cooked vegetables. Sprinkle evenly with lemon peel. Taste and adjust seasoning if necessary.

Makes 8 servings.

Variation:

Replace bok choy with leeks, celery or fennel. Trim away root ends and tattered, tough greenery from leeks; slice in half lengthwise. Proceed as above but extend cooking time to 15 minutes.

Baby Bok Choy Braised in Butter-Lemon Sauce

Don't worry about the amount of butter in this recipe. Most of it is left behind in the pan, yet it adds tremendous flavor during cooking. Save the leftover cooking liquid to toss with vegetables made later in the week.

6	baby bok choy or 1 large bok choy, cut into wedges
3 tbsp (45 mL)	lemon juice
1/4 cup (50 mL)	white wine
1/2 cup (125 mL)	chicken or vegetable broth
1 tsp (5 mL)	granulated sugar
2	shallots, minced
1	3-inch (7.5-cm) piece of lemongrass, chopped in half or 1 tbsp (15 mL) dried lemongrass
1/2 cup (125 mL)	very cold butter, cubed
1 tsp (5 mL)	finely grated lemon peel
	salt and pepper

Preheat oven to 375°F (190°C). Wash baby bok choy well under cold running water. Shake out excess moisture and pat dry. Arrange in a single layer in a casserole dish just large enough to hold bok choy snugly. Reserve.

Combine lemon juice with white wine, broth, sugar, shallots and lemongrass in a saucepan set over medium-high heat. Bring to a boil and cook until reduced to about 1/2 cup (125 mL). Remove the pan from the heat. Whisking constantly, gradually add cubes of butter to sauce, waiting between additions until the butter is completely incorporated. Stir in lemon peel and season with salt and pepper. Pour over bok choy.

Cover tightly with a lid or foil and bake in oven for 35 to 40 minutes or until very tender. Lift out of cooking liquid and serve on a warm platter. Can be made up to 1 day ahead. Discard lemongrass before serving.

Makes 6 servings.

Maple–Glazed Carrots

A fall favorite at our house and perfect as a side dish for Thanksgiving or Christmas dinner.

2 lbs (1 kg)	baby carrots
2 tbsp (30 mL)	butter
1/2 cup (125 mL)	dried cranberries
2 tbsp (30 mL)	pure maple syrup
1 tsp (5 mL)	minced ginger root
1/2 tsp (2 mL)	finely chopped fresh rosemary
1/2 tsp (2 mL)	each salt and pepper

Wash carrots and place in a saucepan. Cover with salted water and bring to a boil. Reduce heat to medium and boil for 3 to 4 minutes or until almost fork tender. Drain well.

Melt butter in a heavy skillet set over medium-high heat. When pan is hot, add carrots and cranberries. Cook, tossing for 3 to 5 minutes or until carrots begin to brown.

Pour in maple syrup. Add ginger, rosemary, salt and pepper. Toss until carrots are fork tender, glossy and caramelized.

Makes 6 to 8 servings.

family favorite

pantry trick

fast but fancy

Tuscan Green Bean Salad

You can almost taste the summer sunshine in this easy to prepare side dish.

1/2 tsp (2 mL)	grated lemon peel
2 tsp (10 mL)	lemon juice
1	small clove garlic, minced
1/4 tsp (1 mL)	each salt and pepper
2 tbsp (30 mL)	extra virgin olive oil
1/3 cup (75 mL)	finely diced aged pecorino or Asiago cheese
1/2 lb (250 g)	green beans

Whisk lemon peel with lemon juice, garlic, salt and pepper. Drizzle in olive oil, whisking constantly. Toss in cheese.

Cut away stem ends from green beans and cut into 2-inch (5-cm) lengths. Blanch in a saucepan of boiling salted water for 3 to 5 minutes or until bright green but still crisp. Drain and refresh under cold running water. Drain well; stir into cheese mixture.

Makes 4 servings.

Plaid Vegetable Toss

family favorite

fast fix

healthier choice

Cutting and cleaning the vegetables ahead of time or buying pre-cut pepper strips makes this colorful recipe a snap to prepare.

2 tbsp (30 mL)	vegetable oil
1	onion, peeled, halved and thinly sliced
1 tsp (5 mL)	granulated sugar
1 tsp (5 mL)	cider vinegar
3	peppers (red, yellow and green)
1/2 lb (250 g)	green beans, tips removed
1	clove garlic, minced
1/2 cup (125 mL)	chicken or vegetable broth
3 tbsp (45 mL)	Worcestershire sauce
1/2 tsp (2 mL)	each salt and pepper

Heat half the oil in a non-stick wok or skillet set over medium heat; add onion and cook, stirring often, for 10 minutes or until very soft; add sugar and vinegar and cook, stirring, for 1 minute. Increase heat to medium-high. Add remaining oil and peppers; cook for 5 minutes or until browned.

Stir in beans, garlic, broth and Worcestershire sauce; cover tightly and cook for about 7 minutes, stirring occasionally. Remove lid and boil for 1 minute or until liquid has evaporated and vegetables are tender. Season with salt and pepper.

Makes 6 to 8 servings.

fast but fancy

fast fix

Sweet and Sour Rainbow Peppers

Serve as a side dish or toss with warm, cooked pasta.

2 tbsp (30 mL)	vegetable oil
1	onion, peeled and thinly sliced
2	cloves garlic, minced
2 tbsp (30 mL)	chopped fresh oregano, or 2 tsp (10 mL) dried oregano
1/2 tsp (2 mL)	each salt and pepper
3	peppers (red, yellow and green), thinly sliced
2 tbsp (30 mL)	red wine vinegar
1 tbsp (15 mL)	liquid honey
1 tbsp (15 mL)	teriyaki sauce or tamari
1 tsp (5 mL)	minced ginger root

Heat half the oil in a wok or non-stick skillet set over medium-high heat. Add the onion and cook, partly covered, stirring occasionally, for 5 minutes. Add garlic, oregano, salt and pepper, and cook for 3 minutes or until onions are very soft.

Add remaining oil to pan and stir in peppers. Cook, stirring often, for 5 minutes or until peppers are browned at the edges but still crunchy. Stir in vinegar, honey, teriyaki or tamari sauce and ginger. Toss for about 1 minute or until peppers are well glazed.

Makes 4 servings.

Sublimely Delicious Caramelized Onions

These onions are great with grilled meats or useful as a building block in other recipes.

2 tbsp (30 mL)	butter
1	Spanish or 3 medium cooking onions, peeled and sliced
1	clove garlic, minced
1 tsp (5 mL)	dried thyme
1/2 tsp (2 mL)	each salt and pepper
2 tbsp (30 mL)	granulated sugar
1/4 cup (50 mL)	sherry
1 tsp (5 mL)	Worcestershire sauce

Melt butter in a large skillet set over medium heat. Add onions, garlic, thyme, salt and pepper. Cook, stirring often, for 10 minutes or until onions are translucent. Increase heat to medium-high and cook, stirring often, for 5 minutes or until onions are just beginning to brown.

Sprinkle in sugar and continue to cook, stirring often, until very brown but not scorched. Add sherry and Worcestershire sauce. Stir to scrape up any brown bits before serving.

Makes 2 to 3 servings.

fast but fancy

pantry plus

Balsamic–Glazed Zucchini, Mushrooms and Tomatoes

This colorful and delicious side dish is also a great filling for pitas or wraps.

2 tbsp (30 mL)	olive or vegetable oil
2 cups (500 mL)	sliced shiitake or other mushrooms
1	zucchini, halved and thinly sliced
2 cups (500 mL)	grape or cherry tomatoes, halved
2 tbsp (30 mL)	balsamic vinegar
1 tsp (5 mL)	dried thyme
1	clove garlic, minced
1/2 tsp (2 mL)	each salt and pepper
pinch	granulated sugar

Heat oil in a deep skillet or wok set over medium-high heat. Add mushrooms and cook, tossing, for 2 to 3 minutes or until beginning to brown. Stir in zucchini slices and cook, tossing, for 2 minutes. Add tomatoes, vinegar, thyme, garlic, salt, pepper and sugar. Cook, tossing, for 2 to 3 minutes or until tomatoes start to split.

Makes 3 to 4 servings.

Desserts and
Sweet Nothings

Any Day Chocolate Pudding

family favorite

pantry plus

Still fast and easy but more delicious than any
store-bought mix.

3 tbsp (45 mL)	cornstarch
2 cups (500 mL)	half-and-half (10%) cream or milk
2/3 cup (150 mL)	granulated sugar
1/2 cup (125 mL)	cocoa
pinch	salt
1/3 cup (75 mL)	hot water
1 tsp (5 mL)	vanilla

Place cornstarch in bowl; whisk in 1/4 cup (50 mL) cream
until smooth. Reserve.

Stir sugar with cocoa and salt in a heavy-bottomed
saucepan; whisk in water until smooth. Set pan over medium heat and cook, stirring constantly, for 3 to 4 minutes or
until mixture comes to a boil. Stir in remaining cream.

Stir reserved cornstarch mixture and, whisking constantly,
add to chocolate mixture. Place over medium-low heat and
cook, stirring constantly, for about 5 minutes or until mixture
comes to a simmer and is thickened. Stir in vanilla; cover
with plastic wrap touching the surface of pudding. Cool to
room temperature.

Makes 4 servings.

Variation:

Puddingsicles: Divide pudding equally between cups in pop-
sicle tray or 9 small paper cups. Stand sticks or spoons in
pudding and place in freezer for at least 1 hour or until
frozen through.

Makes 9 puddingsicles.

light

fast but fancy

Citrus Compote

This easily prepared fruit mixture makes a lovely dessert on its own, a refreshing breakfast treat or a great sauce for plain ice cream, pound cake or cheesecake.

3	oranges
3	red grapefruit
1/4 cup (50 mL)	granulated sugar
2 tbsp (30 mL)	finely chopped crystallized ginger
1 tsp (5 mL)	finely grated lime peel
1/2 cup (125 mL)	orange juice
3/4 tsp (4 mL)	cornstarch
1/4 cup (50 mL)	lightly packed fresh mint leaves

Hold whole oranges on a cutting board and slice away peels and white pith using a sharp knife. Cut between membranes to make segments. Repeat with grapefruit.

Combine oranges and grapefruit with sugar, ginger and lime peel; let stand for 10 minutes. Pour juices off into a small saucepan. Add orange juice; whisk in cornstarch. Bring to boil and simmer, stirring, over medium heat for 2 to 3 minutes or until lightly thickened.

Stir hot syrup back into fruit. Let stand for 15 minutes before serving.

Makes 6 to 8 servings.

Phyllo Tartlet Shells

Fill these easy-to-make pastry cups with ice cream, fruit salad, whipped cream and berries or custard.

2 tbsp (30 mL)	butter
1 tbsp (15 mL)	icing sugar
1/2 tsp (2 mL)	cinnamon (optional)
6	sheets phyllo pastry

fast but fancy

pantry trick

Preheat oven to 375°F (190°C). Melt butter in microwave, in microwave-safe dish, or in small saucepan or skillet set over medium heat. Let cool to room temperature. Stir in icing sugar and cinnamon (if using).

Stack phyllo sheets on top of one another and cut out 3 stacks of 6-inch (15-cm) squares. Discard any scraps of pastry. Cover pastry with a damp clean kitchen towel.

Butter 8 muffin cups lightly. Lightly brush a square of phyllo with butter. Line each muffin cup with a buttered square, folding over edges to fit cup. Repeat this step until each prepared cup is lined with 3 sheets of phyllo.

Bake shells on middle rack of preheated oven until golden brown, about 10 minutes. Using a fork or small palette knife, carefully lift shells out of pan and transfer to a cooling rack.

Makes 12 shells.

family favorite

fast but fancy

make-ahead

Caramel-Topped Chocolate Pudding Cake

A homey dessert that can be served warm from the oven.

Topping:

2 cups (500 mL)	brown sugar
1 1/2 cups (375 mL)	water
2 tbsp (30 mL)	butter

Pudding:

1/4 cup (50 mL)	butter
1 cup (250 mL)	granulated sugar
1/2 cup (125 mL)	cocoa
2	eggs, beaten
2 cups (500 mL)	all-purpose flour
1 tsp (5 mL)	salt
1 tbsp (15 mL)	baking powder
2/3 cup (150 mL)	warm milk

Topping:

Combine brown sugar with water and butter in a medium saucepan set over medium-high heat. Bring to a boil and simmer for 5 minutes. Cool slightly.

Cake:

Preheat oven to 350°F (180°C). Grease a 9 x 13-inch (3 L) baking dish and set aside. In a bowl, using an electric mixer, combine butter with sugar and beat until fluffy. Beat in cocoa, then eggs.

Blend flour with salt and baking powder. Add to egg mixture in three additions, alternating with warm milk and scraping down the sides of the bowl each time. Scrape mixture into prepared pan and smooth top. Slowly pour sauce mixture over prepared batter.

Bake on center rack in preheated oven for 30 minutes or until a tester inserted in center of cake comes out clean. Place on a rack and cool for 10 minutes. Serve warm, cutting cake into squares and turning over so that sauce, which will have sunk to the bottom, is on top. Scrape any sauce which remains in pan over top of pudding and spread evenly. Serve warm or reheated.

Makes 8 to 10 servings.

pantry plus

fast but fancy

I Spy Skillet Apple Pie

The classic French dessert, tarte Tatin, uses puff pastry but this version can be made with short pastry, too.

6	peeled, cored, thickly sliced firm apples, such as Spy or Spartan
1/2 cup (125 mL)	raisins (optional)
2 tbsp (30 mL)	lemon juice
1 tsp (5 mL)	cinnamon
1/4 cup (50 mL)	butter
1/2 cup (125 mL)	granulated sugar
1 8 oz (250 g) pkg	thawed, frozen puff pastry or thawed frozen pastry shell, rolled to fit over skillet

Preheat oven to 425°F (220°C). Toss apples with raisins (if using), lemon juice and cinnamon. Melt butter in a 12-inch (30-cm) ovenproof skillet set over medium-high heat. Sprinkle in the sugar and stir to combine. Arrange apples in pan. Reduce heat to medium and cook, without stirring, for 15 minutes or until a golden caramel has formed in the pan.

Spread pastry over top of fruit so that apples are completely covered. Fold over the edge of the pastry to fit pan snugly. Transfer pie to preheated oven. Bake for 20 to 25 minutes, if using puff pastry, or until pastry is golden and crisp. Or, if using short pastry, reduce baking time by about 5 minutes. Turn pie out onto a large platter. Spoon any remaining juices over top of pie.

Makes 8 servings.

Tips: Serve with whipped cream, vanilla ice cream or thinly sliced pieces of aged cheddar cheese.

If using frozen apple slices, defrost completely and drain well before adding to pan.

Variation:

Pear and cranberry: Substitute 6 large, firm pears for apples and dried cranberries for raisins.

Crumb-Topped Cherry Cheesecake

healthier choice

pantry trick

This version of a traditional cheesecake is much lighter than the original but still silky and satisfying.

2 8 oz (250 g) pkgs	light brick-style cream cheese, softened
1 cup (250 mL)	granulated sugar
1 tbsp (15 mL)	finely grated lemon peel
1 tsp (5 mL)	vanilla
3	eggs
1/2 cup (125 mL)	graham wafer crumbs
1 cup (250 mL)	cherry or other fruit pie filling

Preheat oven to 350°F (180°C). In a large mixing bowl, combine cream cheese, sugar, lemon peel and vanilla. Beat on low until mixture is very smooth. Add eggs and blend well.

Scrape mixture into a 9-inch (23-cm) pie plate that has been sprayed with vegetable oil. Sprinkle graham crumbs evenly over top. Bake in preheated oven for 30 minutes. Turn off oven and cool cheesecake in oven for 30 minutes. Refrigerate for at least 4 hours or overnight. Slice and serve each portion topped with 2 tbsp (30 mL) cherry or other fruit pie filling.

Makes 8 servings.

One-Bowl Chocolate Birthday Cake

This eggless, milkless and butter-free layer cake can be thrown together even when you feel like you have nothing in the house.

3 cups (750 mL)	all-purpose flour
2 cups (500 mL)	granulated sugar
1/2 cup (125 mL)	unsweetened cocoa powder
2 tsp (10 mL)	baking soda
1 tsp (5 mL)	salt
1 tsp (5 mL)	instant coffee granules
1/2 cup (125 mL)	corn oil
2 tbsp (30 mL)	white vinegar
1 tsp (5 mL)	vanilla
2 1/2 cups (625 mL)	cold water

Preheat oven to 350°F (180°C). Using a fork, blend flour with sugar, cocoa, baking soda, salt and coffee.

Pour oil, vinegar, vanilla and water into bowl over dry ingredients. Mix, using an electric mixer on low speed, until well combined.

Line bottoms of 2 lightly greased 8-inch (20-cm) round baking pans with parchment or wax paper. Scrape batter into pans. Place on center rack in preheated oven. Bake for 30 to 35 minutes or until springy when lightly touched in the center. Cool on a rack for 5 minutes. Turn out, remove paper and cool completely.

Creamy Chocolate Frosting

2 cups (500 mL)	semisweet or milk chocolate chips
1 cup (250 mL)	sour cream

Heat chocolate chips in a microwave-safe bowl for 1 minute. Stir until smooth. Stir in sour cream. Beat, using an electric mixer, until smooth. Cover and refrigerate for about 15 minutes or until mixture is the consistency of smooth peanut butter.

Spread enough frosting over bottom layer of cake to coat thickly. Top with remaining cake layer. Spread remaining frosting evenly over entire cake and decorate as desired.

Variations:

Five-spice chocolate cake: Omit coffee granules and add 1 tbsp (15 mL) Chinese five-spice powder to dry ingredients.

Mocha: Increase coffee granules in cake to 1 tbsp (15 mL) and add 1 tbsp (15 mL) coffee-flavored liqueur to icing.

Turtle-Topped Mini Mud Pies

As fudgy and decadent as you can get. Pour a big glass of cold milk and enjoy!

8 oz (500 g)	unsweetened chocolate, chopped
1/4 cup (50 mL)	butter
1/4 tsp (1 mL)	salt
1 1/2 cups (375 mL)	granulated sugar
3	eggs
2 tsp (10 mL)	vanilla
1 cup (250 mL)	all-purpose flour
2 1/2 cups (625 mL)	chopped chocolate-covered caramel candies, about 6 pkgs
1/2 cup (125 mL)	pecan pieces
	chocolate or caramel sauce

Spray eight 1/2-cup (125-mL) ramekins or custard cups with cooking spray; reserve. Preheat oven to 350°F (180°C).

Melt chocolate and butter, stirring occasionally, in a heavy saucepan set over low heat. Stir in salt. Cool slightly. Stir in sugar and eggs, adding one at a time. Stir in vanilla. Gradually stir in flour until well combined.

Divide batter evenly among prepared cups and spread out. Top evenly with the chopped candies and nuts; place pans on a baking tray. Bake in preheated oven for 20 to 25 minutes or until a tester inserted in center of brownies comes out with just a few moist crumbs attached. Cool for 5 minutes on a rack. Run a butter knife around edge of each dish. Turn out onto a wax paper-lined plate and turn back out onto a rack to cool. Serve with chocolate or caramel sauce.

Makes 8 servings.

Tip: This recipe can also be made in an 8-inch (22-cm) square pan. Extend baking time to 30 minutes. Cut into squares or bars when almost cool.

Variation:

German Chocolate Topping:

This topping makes a great substitute for the caramel-chocolate bar topping called for above. Bake the mud pies with no topping and add this mixture when cool.

¼ cup (50 mL)	butter
¼ cup (50 mL)	brown sugar
¼ cup (950 mL)	milk
1	egg
1 cup (250 mL)	finely chopped pecans
1 cup (250 mL)	sweetened featherflake coconut
1 tsp (5 mL)	vanilla

Combine butter, sugar, milk and egg in a saucepan. Cook, stirring, over medium-low heat until mixture comes to a boil and thickens, about 5 minutes. Stir in pecans, coconut and vanilla. Divide evenly and spread over baked chocolate mud pies.

Lemongrass Crème Caramels

Although crème caramel, or flan, is popular in Europe and Latin America, its texture and ingredients lend themselves to being paired with Asian flavors like lemongrass.

Caramel:

3/4 cup (175 mL)	granulated sugar
1/4 cup (50 mL)	water

Custard:

2 cups (500 mL)	homogenized milk
3/4 cup (175 mL)	granulated sugar
5	stalks lemongrass, chopped into 1/4-inch (5-mm) pieces
4	eggs
4	egg yolks
1 tsp (5 mL)	vanilla
pinch	salt

Tip: To make preparation easier, chop lemongrass in a mini-chopper or food processor.

Place sugar in a small, heavy saucepan; pour water over top. Set pan over medium heat and cook without boiling or stirring, but gently swirling pan by the handle, until a clear syrup forms. Increase heat to high and bring the syrup to a rolling boil. Cook until syrup is amber, about 10 minutes. Quickly divide the caramel among 8 ramekins or custard cups; immediately tilt dishes to spread caramel evenly in bottoms. Reserve.

Custard:

Heat milk, sugar and lemongrass until steaming with bubbles just beginning to form around edges of pan. Cover and let stand for 15 minutes. Preheat oven to 325°F (160°C).

Whisk eggs with yolks, vanilla and salt. Strain lemongrass out of milk mixture and discard. Gently whisk milk into egg mixture. Pour into caramel-lined dishes and place in roasting pan. Fill roaster with boiling water to halfway up sides of ramekins. Cover with foil and poke top a few times to make vent holes.

Bake in 325°F (160°C) oven for 25 to 30 minutes or until set but still jiggly. Remove from water bath and cool. Refrigerate for about 2 hours or for up to 2 days.

Dip bottom of ramekins in hot water and run a knife around the edge. Turn out onto plates.

Makes 8 servings.

Variations:

Large flan: Pour the caramel into an 8-cup (2 L) glass dish. Cook for 50 to 60 minutes.

Tahitian vanilla: Replace lemongrass with a Tahitian, Veracruz or other vanilla bean that has been cut in half lengthwise.

family favorite

pantry trick

Caramel Corn

Be careful: this caramel corn is a little too easy to make, if you know what I mean!

1	bag microwave popping corn, about 8 cups (2 L) popped
1 cup (250 mL)	packed brown sugar
1/2 cup (125 mL)	butter
1/4 cup (50 mL)	corn syrup
1/2 tsp (2 mL)	baking soda

Place popcorn in a large roasting pan; reserve.

Combine brown sugar, butter and corn syrup in small, heavy-bottomed saucepan. Cook, stirring, over medium heat until mixture comes to a boil. Continue to cook for 2 minutes without stirring.

Remove pan from heat and quickly whisk in baking soda. Drizzle over popcorn mixture and stir to coat evenly.

Place in 300°F (150°C) oven for 15 minutes; stir well and return to oven for 5 minutes. Stir again and cool in pan for 5 minutes.

Makes about 8 cups.

Variation:

Chocolate: Stir 1/2 cup (125 mL) unsweetened cocoa powder into brown sugar mixture.

Elegant Chocolate Clusters

Great as gifts or as part of a sweet tray, these bite-size treats can be made with whatever nuts and dried fruit you have on hand.

1/2 cup (125 mL)	corn syrup
1 cup (250 mL)	whole, unblanched almonds or hazelnuts
1 cup (250 mL)	roasted cashews, peanuts or pecan halves
8 oz (500 g)	bittersweet or milk chocolate, chopped
1/2 cup (125 mL)	crystallized ginger or other dried fruit, cut into long, thin sticks

Preheat oven to 350°F (180°C).

Mix corn syrup with nuts in a saucepan set over medium heat; bring to a boil. Lift nuts out of corn syrup, leaving excess behind, and spread evenly on a foil-lined baking sheet.

Bake in oven for 15 minutes or until caramelized. Cool completely; break apart any nuts that are stuck together.

Melt chocolate in microwave for 2 minutes on medium power; stir until smooth. Place a cookie sheet in the freezer until cold; line with waxed paper.

Tip: If chocolate begins to thicken, soften in microwave for 10 seconds

Drop half-teaspoonfuls (2 mL) of chocolate onto cold tray. While still soft, arrange one of each type of nut and a piece of fruit on each chocolate round. Let cool completely. Can be stored in a tightly covered container in refrigerator for up to 1 month.

Makes 5 dozen chocolates.

Millennium Crispy Bars

These marshmallow cereal bars have improved flavor, fiber and nutrients over traditional rice cereal bars due to the cranberries and green pumpkinseeds.

1/4 cup (50 mL)	butter
1 8 oz (250 g) pkg	marshmallows, about 40
1 tsp (5 mL)	vanilla
5 cups (1.25 L)	crisp rice cereal
1 cup (250 mL)	dried cranberries or raisins
1/2 cup (125 mL)	raw green pumpkin seeds

Spray a 13 x 9-inch (3 L) baking dish lightly with vegetable oil; set aside.

Melt butter in a saucepan set over medium-low heat. Stir in marshmallows, a handful at a time, until smooth. Remove from heat and stir in vanilla. Add crisp rice, cranberries or raisins and green pumpkin seeds, stirring until evenly combined. Press into prepared dish. Cool completely and cut into rectangles.

Makes 20 bars.

Crunchy Cloud Cookies

healthier choice

fast fix

Satisfy your sweet tooth quickly and easily with these light cookies. Lots of crunch and flavor without lots of calories from fat!

2 cups (500 mL)	cornflakes
2/3 cup (150 mL)	toasted, sliced almonds
1/2 cup (125 mL)	dried cranberries or raisins
2	egg whites
pinch	cream of tartar
1/2 cup (125 mL)	granulated sugar
1 oz (28 g)	semisweet chocolate, melted (optional)

Stir cornflakes with almonds and cranberries or raisins; reserve. Preheat oven to 300°F (150°C).

Using an electric mixer, beat egg whites until foamy; add cream of tartar and continue to beat for 1 to 2 minutes or until soft peaks form. Still beating, gradually add sugar; beat until stiff.

Fold cornflake mixture gently into egg whites, using a rubber spatula. Drop heaping teaspoonfuls of batter onto a parchment-lined baking sheet. Bake in preheated oven for about 20 minutes or until cookies are very lightly browned. Cool completely; drizzle with chocolate (if using). Store in airtight container up to 1 week.

Makes about 30 cookies.

family favorite

make-ahead

Frozen Asset Cookies

These make-ahead frozen cookie dough recipes are ideal for baking as you need them.

1. Classic Chocolate Chunk Cookies

A favorite with kids of all ages.

1 cup (250 mL)	butter
1 cup (250 mL)	packed brown sugar
1/2 cup (125 mL)	granulated sugar
2	eggs
2 tsp (10 mL)	vanilla
2 3/4 cups (675 mL)	all-purpose flour
1 tsp (5 mL)	baking soda
1/4 tsp (1 mL)	salt
2 cups (500 mL)	semisweet or bittersweet chocolate chips

Cream butter in a large bowl. Beat in brown sugar and granulated sugar until very smooth. Beat in eggs, one at a time, until combined. Stir in vanilla. Add flour, baking soda and salt. Stir until well combined. Add chocolate chips and mix until combined.

Use a tiny (1 oz/28 mL) ice cream scoop or a melon baller to scoop balls of cookie dough. If necessary, roll between lightly floured hands to make evenly shaped balls (if you leave jagged edges the cookies will bake unevenly). Place on a wax paper-lined tray and set in the freezer for 15 minutes or until firm. Transfer to a zip-top plastic bag or other airtight container and reserve in freezer until ready to bake. (Alternatively, roll dough into long cylinders about 2 inches/ 5 cm wide then slice thickly before baking, at 350°F/180°C for 10 minutes.)

To bake: Preheat oven to 350°F (180°C). Spread the frozen cookie nuggets out on a lightly greased baking sheet at least 2 inches (5 cm) apart. Bake for 10 to 12 minutes or until edges are crisp and bottoms are golden brown.

Makes about 6 dozen cookies.

2. Tuxedo Cookies

Choose high-quality white chocolate for best results.

1 cup (250 mL)	softened butter
1 cup (250 mL)	dark brown sugar
3/4 cup (175 mL)	granulated sugar
3	eggs
1 tsp (5 mL)	vanilla
2 1/2 cups (625 mL)	all-purpose flour
1/2 cup (125 mL)	cocoa powder
1 tsp (5 mL)	baking soda
1/2 tsp (2 mL)	salt
2 cups (500 mL)	white chocolate chips or chunks

Prepare using the method for Classic Chocolate Chunk Cookies (page 186).

3. Old-Fashioned Oatmeal Cookies

These cookies are so perfect with a cup of tea that I sometimes bake two or three (okay, I admit one day it was four) for myself in the afternoon when I'm working at my computer.

1 cup (250 mL)	softened butter
3 cups (750 mL)	brown sugar
2	eggs
1 tsp (5 mL)	vanilla
2 cups (500 mL)	all-purpose flour
1 tsp (5 mL)	baking powder
1 tsp (5 mL)	cinnamon
1/2 tsp (2 mL)	salt
2 cups (500 mL)	rolled oats
1 cup (250 mL)	unsweetened shredded coconut
1 cup (250 mL)	sultana or other raisins

Prepare using the method for Classic Chocolate Chunk Cookies (page 186).

4. Peanut Butter Toffee Crunch Cookies

Unlike some peanut butter cookies, this slice and bake version bakes up to be crisp.

3/4 cup (175 mL)	crunchy peanut butter
3/4 cup (175 mL)	softened butter
1 1/3 cups (325 mL)	granulated sugar
1	egg
1 tsp (5 mL)	vanilla
2 cups (500 mL)	all-purpose flour
3/4 tsp (4 mL)	baking soda
pinch	salt
2/3 cup (150 mL)	crunchy toffee baking bits

Beat peanut butter with butter in a large bowl. Add sugar and beat until smooth. Beat in egg and vanilla. Add flour, baking soda and salt. Use a wooden spoon to stir into butter mixture until well combined. Stir in toffee bits.

Divide dough into thirds and roll into 8-inch (20-cm) logs, using a piece of waxed paper as a guide, if necessary. Remove paper and tightly wrap each log individually in plastic wrap. Freeze for 10 minutes; shape log into a perfect cylinder. Return to freezer for at least 2 hours or until very firm. (Logs can be frozen for up to 1 month.)

To bake: Preheat oven to 375°F (190°C). Lightly spray a cookie sheet with cooking spray. Use a serrated knife to cut frozen or chilled dough into slices about 1/4-inch (4-mm) thick. Place on baking sheet and bake for 8 to 10 minutes or until golden. Remove to a rack and cool.

Makes about 7 dozen cookies.

5. Orange Butterscotch Wafers

These crisp cookies are perfect for dunking.

1 cup (250 mL)	softened butter
1/2 cup (125 mL)	packed brown sugar
1/2 cup (125 mL)	granulated sugar
1	egg
1 tsp (5 mL)	vanilla
2 1/3 cups (575 mL)	all-purpose flour
1/2 tsp (2 mL)	baking soda
1/2 tsp (2 mL)	salt
1 tbsp (15 mL)	finely grated orange peel
3/4 cup (175 mL)	toasted, finely chopped hazelnuts or almonds

Prepare using the same method as Peanut Butter Toffee Crunch Cookies (page 189).

Saucepan Brownies

family favorite

pantry trick

No bowl and only one spoon to wash—now, that's easy!

4 oz (125 g)	chopped unsweetened chocolate
1/2 cup (125 mL)	butter
1 1/2 cups (375 mL)	granulated sugar
1 tsp (5 mL)	vanilla
1/4 tsp (1 mL)	salt
3	eggs
1 cup (250 mL)	all-purpose flour

Place chocolate and butter in a saucepan set over low heat. Heat, stirring often, until chocolate is almost melted. Remove from heat and stir until smooth. Cool slightly. Preheat oven to 350°F (180°C).

Stir sugar, vanilla and salt into chocolate mixture. Stir in eggs, one at a time. Blend in flour until well combined. Scrape mixture into a greased 9-inch (23-cm) square pan or 7 x 11-inch (1.5 L) baking dish. Bake for 30 to 35 minutes or until a tester inserted in the center comes out with just a few crumbs attached. Cool in pan on a rack. Slice into bars.

Makes 24 bars.

Red Wine Milkshake

The syrup for this milkshake can be made ahead and refrigerated. Use it as a sauce for pound cake, sundaes or fresh fruit, too.

2 cups (500 mL)	red wine
1/2 cup (125 mL)	granulated sugar
1/4 cup (50 mL)	orange juice
3	whole cloves
1	cinnamon stick
1 1/2 cups (375 mL)	vanilla ice cream
1 1/2 cups (375 mL)	milk

Combine red wine, sugar, orange juice, cloves and cinnamon in a small saucepan. Bring to a boil and cook over medium-high heat for 15 to 20 minutes or until reduced to about 3/4 cup (175 mL). Strain out cloves and cinnamon and cool completely. Refrigerate until cold.

Combine 1/4 cup (50 mL) chilled syrup with 1/2 cup (125 mL) vanilla ice cream and 1/2 cup (125 mL) milk in a blender or food processor for each milk shake. Blend on high and pour into a tall glass.

Makes 3 shakes.

Fuss-Free Chocolate-Caramel Shortbread Bars

Prepare and bake 5 dozen cookies in less than 45 minutes!

family favorite

fast fix

1 tbsp (15 mL)	instant coffee granules
1 tsp (5 mL)	hot water
2 cups (500 mL)	butter, softened
1 cup (250 mL)	granulated sugar
4 cups (1 L)	all-purpose flour
1½ cups (375 mL)	chopped chocolate-covered crisp toffee bars, such as Skor

Preheat oven to 350°F (180°C). Dissolve coffee in water. Beat butter, coffee and sugar until fluffy. Stir flour with candy in seporate bowl. Mix into butter mixture 1/2 cup (125 mL) at a time until combined.

Press dough into an 11 x 17-inch (27.5 x 42.5-cm) rimmed baking sheet. Bake in preheated oven for about 25 minutes or until lightly browned. Remove from oven. Slice into bars using a sharp knife. Cool completely in pan on rack. Store in an airtight container for up to 1 week or freeze for up to 1 month.

Makes about 60 cookies.

fast but fancy

family favorite

Bourbon–Caramel Blondies

Too yummy to resist, these dense treats are perfect for bake sales.

1/2 cup (125 mL)	butter, softened
1 1/4 cups (300 mL)	lightly packed brown sugar
2	eggs
3 tbsp (45 mL)	bourbon or 1 tsp (5 mL) vanilla
1 1/2 cups (375 mL)	all-purpose flour
1/4 tsp (1 mL)	salt
1 cup (250 mL)	toffee or butterscotch chips
2 oz (60 g)	bittersweet chocolate, melted

Preheat oven to 350°F (180°C). Spray an 8-inch (2 L) baking pan with cooking spray and reserve. Beat butter with sugar until fluffy. Beat in eggs, one at a time. Stir in bourbon or vanilla.

Use a fork to combine flour and salt in a separate bowl. Stir in toffee or butterscotch chips and add to butter mixture in 2 additions. Spread batter into prepared pan. Bake in center of preheated oven for 40 minutes or until blondies pull away from the sides of the pan but center is still moist. Cool on a rack.

Drizzle melted chocolate from the tines of a fork all over cooked blondies. Chill for 10 minutes to set chocolate. Slice into bars.

Makes 20 bars.

Index

About the Author

Dana McCauley is one of those rare people who seems exactly suited to her profession. The unbeatable combination of a Bachelor of Arts in English from Queen's University and a successful year at the Stratford Chefs School paved the way for her to gain prominence in her field by writing cookbooks, communicating about food and accurately forecasting burgeoning food trends.

Under the banner of Dana McCauley & Associates, Dana is the freelance food editor for *Homemaker's* magazine and a trend analyst for many international food companies. She writes *Topline Trends*, a quarterly e-mail newsletter, conducts cooking classes and speaks to audiences at venues such as the Smithsonian Institute and trade shows.

An accomplished cookbook author, Dana has already published two other titles: the bestselling *Last Dinner on the Titanic* (co-written with Rick Archbold) and *Noodles Express*. As a time crunched mom, Dana considers her book, *Pantry Raid*, a necessary weeknight tool for her own kitchen counter as well as for her readers.

Born in Newmarket, Ontario, Dana's family lived in many places including North York, Richmond Hill and Vancouver. Growing up, Dana always pictured herself working in the kitchen; in fact, she has an amusing photograph of herself at age six using her Easy Bake oven in mismatched plaid hot pants and a boldly striped shirt. She now lives in Richmond Hill with her young son Oliver, and her husband Martin Kouprie, chef and co-owner of Pangaea Restaurant in Toronto. Although her family chides her about being a workaholic, Dana considers herself a literary buff, a student of pop culture and an expert furniture re-arranger.